CATALOGUE

OF THE

PREHISTORIC ANTIQUITIES

FROM

ADICHANALLUR AND PERUMBAIR

CATALOGUE

OF THE

PREHISTORIC ANTIQUITIES

FROM

ADICHANALLUR AND PERUMBAIR

BY

ALEXANDER REA, F. S. A. (Scot.)

GYAN

Published by

GYAN

Gyan Publishing House
5, Ansari Road
Daryaganj, New Delhi-110002
Phone: 011-47034999, 9811692060
E-mail: books@gyanbooks.com

Distribution Network
gyanbooks.com
India, USA, Canada, UK, Australia

ISBN: 978-93-6208-774-4 (PB)
First Published, 1915

2nd Impression 2024

Printed at: Gyan Press, Delhi.

CATALOGUE OF THE PREHISTORIC ANTIQUITIES FROM ADICHANALLUR AND PERUMBAIR
Author: ALEXANDER REA

CATALOGUE

OF THE

PREHISTORIC ANTIQUITIES

FROM

ĀDICHANALLŪR AND PERUMBAIR.

BY

ALEXANDER REA, F.S.A. (SCOT.),

Superintendent, Archæological Survey, Southern Circle (Retired);
Honorary Assistant Superintendent, Government Museum,
Madras.

MADRAS:
PRINTED BY THE SUPERINTENDENT, GOVERNMENT PRESS.

PRICE, 1 *rupee* 8 *annas.*] 1915. [2 *shillings* 3 *pence.*

PREFACE.

THE two important collections which form the subject of this catalogue were brought together as the result of excavations conducted by Mr. A. Rea, formerly Superintendent of the Archæological Survey of India, Southern Circle, and are exhibited in an extension of the Prehistoric Gallery of the Madras Government Museum which was specially erected for their accommodation. Mr. Rea, for some time prior to his retirement from the service of Government in October 1913, was placed on special duty in connection with the archæological collections in the Museum, and the present catalogue is one of the results of his work.

By far the more extensive of the two finds is that from Ādichanallūr and other localities in the Tinnevelly or most southern district of the Madras Presidency. The Ādichanallūr site was first brought to notice in 1876, when it was visited by Dr. Jagor of Berlin, who secured a considerable number of articles for the Berlin Museum für Völkerkunde. Further explorations were conducted in the winter of 1903–1904, by M. Louis Lapicque of Paris, which resulted in additional collections, and as a result of their examination M. Lapicque arrived at the conclusion that the remains belonged to a Proto-Dravidian race. A detailed investigation of the sites was conducted by Mr. Rea, at intervals from 1899 to 1905, when the present collection and a large number of duplicates were obtained. While admitting that the burial-grounds might be of great antiquity, Mr. Rea was on the whole disposed to think that they were of Pāndyan origin and might even have been in use after the commencement of the Christian era.

The burial-ground at Ādichanallūr covers an area of one hundred and fourteen acres and is the most extensive yet discovered in South India. The funeral urns were deposited either singly, or more rarely in pairs, in pits excavated in the solid rock or in the gravelly soil. In most cases only a selection of bones appears to have been interred, and as there are no evidences of cremation it seems probable that only portions of the body were placed in each urn, a theory which is supported by the small size of many of the latter and the narrowness of their mouths.

The burial urns and other articles of pottery which constitute the majority of the objects found at Ādichanallūr, do not appear to differ in any important respect from similar finds made in various other South Indian localities. Many of the smaller vessels, some of which it may be remarked closely resemble objects of prehistoric pottery found in Egypt (*cf.* v. Bissing, Sitzgsb. d. Königl. Bayer. Akad. d. Wissensch. philos.-philol. u. hist. Kl., Jahrg. 1911, 6 Abh.) exhibit a characteristic red and black polished surface, which was the result of friction and not of a true fused glaze. The smaller articles consist for the most part of ordinary domestic utensils, together with stands of various kinds on which the vessels requiring support were placed. Comparatively little applied decoration is found and that practically confined to the large urns. The domestic utensils were found both in the interior of the urns and outside them, and as many contained rice husks they were perhaps originally receptacles for grain intended to serve as food for the spirits of the dead.

The most interesting of the Tinnevelly finds are, however, the objects in metal, as they exist in great variety, a considerable amount of skill has been exercised in their manufacture, and many are of hitherto unknown design. The majority are of iron, but a fair number occur in bronze, and the uses to which some of the more complicated articles were put are still somewhat conjectural. The only objects discovered in any of the precious metals are oval frontlets of gold leaf, which were probably tied round the forehead in the case of certain of the dead, possibly those of rank or importance.

The iron articles include swords, daggers, spear-heads, arrow-heads and other weapons used in warfare or in hunting, agricultural implements resembling the modern "mammutti," though it is by no means certain that they were originally fixed at right angles to the shaft, and others more difficult to classify such as tridents two or three feet in length, and the peculiar "hangers" probably used for the suspension of iron saucer lamps of which several were found. The weapons and implements appear to have been inserted point downwards in the earth by the persons present at the interment.

Though much fewer in number, the bronze articles are executed with higher skill than those in iron, and unlike the latter which appear to have been made for purely utilitarian purposes, comprise objects which can only have been intended for ornament, and thus afford the best available evidence of the art of the people who fashioned them. This particularly applies to the numerous representations of animals, usually arranged in radiating rows on complicated metal frame-works some of which apparently formed supports for spherical vessels, while others were elaborately decorated lids. Although the workmanship is crude the animals can be readily identified, and special attention may be directed to a spirited representation of a village dog (No. 105), which, although found isolated, probably formed part of one of these peculiar ornaments. It is worthy of note that the cow and other animals specially distinctive of Hindu mythology are not represented. The buffalo appears to have been most generally selected, and this animal still plays an all-important part in the religious ritual of the Todas, a Dravidian tribe long isolated on the Nilgiri Hills. In the room adjoining that in which the present collection is exhibited, will be found numerous objects in pottery, iron and bronze, discovered by Mr. J. W. Breeks, a former Commissioner of the Nilgiris, in the cairns and barrows of those hills, which this investigator believed to be of early Toda origin (*cf.* "An Account of the Primitive Tribes and Monuments of the Nilagiris. By

J. W. Breeks. London, 1873," and "Government Museum, Madras. Catalogue of the Prehistoric Antiquities. By R. Bruce-Foote. Madras, 1901"). The Nilgiri animal figures, which include the buffalo, exist only in clay and are distinctly coarse in execution; while they were probably used in most cases to decorate the lids of vessels, the nature of the material used prevented any attempt at elaboration in design, such as occurs in the Ādichanallūr lids. In other respects, however, there is no great similarity between the Tinnevelly and Nilgiri exhibits. The remaining articles in bronze from Ādichanallūr comprise personal ornaments and domestic utensils, including the peculiar "sieve cups" or strainers, but no weapons or implements appear to have been fashioned in this metal.

The human remains found in the urns include a number of skulls and other bones which are still in a fair state of preservation. Mr. E. Thurston's measurements of six of the most perfect skulls are quoted by Mr. Rea, and it is hoped that a detailed account of the osteological specimens will eventually be published.

The second and smaller collection, included in the present catalogue, comprises prehistoric remains from the neighbourhood of Perumbāir, in the Chingleput district, about fifty miles south of Madras, obtained by Mr. Rea, as the result of excavations which he conducted from 1904 to 1908. Here, as in many other localities in the Madras Presidency, the ancient burial sites are indicated on the surface by circles of rough stone boulders, and in the centre of each circle at a depth of from two to seven feet, was found either a pyriform urn or an earthenware cist. The urns belong to a type of which the Museum previously possessed specimens from various South Indian localities, while the more unusual cists resemble those found at Pallavaram, eleven miles south of Madras, but differ from the latter in generally possessing a greater number of legs or supports. The subsidiary articles, which were found both inside and near the burial receptacles, consist for the most part of pottery, but stone objects, mostly suitable for grinding, a few iron implements and some chank shell ornaments were also discovered. The pottery is of a distinctly coarser fabric than that of the Ādichanallūr find.

The long earthenware cists or sarcophagi, of which seven are exhibited, appear originally to have been furnished with perforated arched lids, two of which are preserved *in situ.* The nature of the soil at Perumbāir has not been favourable for the preservation either of the pottery or of the human remains, and the bones are all in a more or less fragmentary condition In one case Mr. Rea obtained evidence of what appeared to be a comparatively modern interment in this prehistoric cemetery, and the theory that the site continued to be so used in later times, is supported by the discovery of a small stone image of Ganēśa which was found buried in the soil.

Illustrated articles by Mr. Rea on the Ādichanallūr antiquities, will be found in the Annual Reports of the Archæological Survey of India, for 1902–03 and 1903–04, and on those from Perumbāir in the Report for 1908–09.

J. R. HENDERSON,

October 1914. *Supt., Madras Govt. Museum.*

GLOSSARY OF INDIAN TERMS USED.

1. *Agal.*—Small saucer-like lamp, with a beak for the wick.
2. *Bōgini.*—Small cup-like vessel.
3. *Jādi.*—Globular vessel resembling a jar.
4. *Kalayam.*—Small globular vessel, with narrow mouth; for holding oil, etc.
5. *Kinnam.*—Small wide-mouthed vessel for holding liquids.
6. *Kuḷam.*—Vessel used for bringing water from a distance, with raised neck.
7. *Kuḍuvai.*—Elongated vessel with a narrow mouth; used for preparing broths.
8. *Kuṇḍān.*—Broad-mouthed globular vessel for the storage of liquids.
9. *Kuṇḍu Bōgini.*—Similar to No. 2 but smaller.
10. *Kuṇḍu Monthai.*—Tumbler-like, with a flat or conical base, wide mouth and depressed neck; for holding liquids.
11. *Maḍakku.*—Similar to No. 8, but mouth broader and thick rim; for preparing soups, etc.
12. *Maikkinnam.*—Small cup for keeping "*mai,*" i.e., a black ointment for the eye.
13. *Mammuṭṭi.*—This resembles a modern spade, but has the blade at right angles to the handle.
14. *Marakkāl.*—Similar to No. 8, but higher; for measuring grain.
15. *Maravai.*—Elongated vessel for the storage of fluids.
16. *Mondai.*—Vessel with a flat base, wide mouth and raised neck; used for storing liquids.
17. *Mūḍi.*—Lid or covering.
18. *Mūkku Kinnam.*—Same as No. 5, but with a spout.
19. *Mūsai.*—Similar to No. 15, but sometimes longer.
20. *Pāli.*—A raised ringstand-like vessel, used in Hindu families on marriage occasions for the sowing of different seeds.
21. *Pallāi.*—Similar to No. 4, but larger in size; for holding a large quantity of liquid.
22. *Pānai.*—Large globular vessel, for the storage of water or other household necessaries.
23. *Śaruvaśaṭṭi.*—Small wide-mouthed vessel, used in Hindu families for cooking purposes.
24. *Śaṭṭi.*—Same as No. 23, but larger in size.
25. *Śithai.*—Resembles No. 8, but globular and slightly elongated at the bottom, with narrow mouth.
26. *Śombu.*—A small globular vessel, with raised neck; for holding liquids.
27. *Śoppu.*—Toys of different kinds and shapes.
28. *Śorakkāi-lōṭṭā.*—A tumbler with a large central depressed groove; for holding water for drinking purposes.
29. *Śūlam.*—This resembles a single blade of a trident.
30. *Tāḷam.*—Circular or oval plate for holding cooked rice.
31. *Tavalai.*—Similar to No. 26, but with broader mouth and body; for keeping water, etc.
32. *Triśūlam.*—Trident.
33. *Tōṇḍi.*—Similar to No. 22, but with conical bottom and narrow neck; for bringing water from a distance.
34. *Uruḷi.*—Broad-mouthed vessel for cooking purposes, etc.
35. *Vaali.*—Same as No 34, but larger in size.

LIST OF ABBREVIATIONS.

Fig.	Figure.
Pl.	Plate.
L.	Length.
B.	Breadth.
D.	Diameter.
H.	Height.
R.	Radius.
M/D	Mouth Diameter.
⊙ce	Circumference.
⊙ce at m.b.	Circumference at middle belt.
D.G.'s Annual	Annual Report of the Archæological Survey of India.
Annual Report of A.D.	Annual Report of the Archæological Survey, Southern Circle.

CONTENTS.

TINNEVELLY PREHISTORIC ANTIQUITIES.

INTRODUCTION.*

The site at Àdichanallūr stands on the right bank of the Tāmbaraparni river, about two miles west of the town of Srivaikuntam in the Tinnevelly district. It was first brought to notice in 1876, when it was visited by Dr. Jagor of Berlin, accompanied by Mr. Stuart, the Acting Collector of Tinnevelly, and by the District Engineer.

The Collector, in a letter to Government,† said:—"We commenced excavations in the side of a hill consisting chiefly of quartz gravel with boulders of the same material and resting on gneiss rock and within a superficial area of twenty-five or thirty square yards, we discovered from twenty to thirty baked earthen pots varying in size from three feet nine by three feet six down to ten inches either way, of very various shapes, and of shapes in most cases more elegant and of a better manufacture than any one sees at the present day in the bazaars.

"These pots, when examined, were found to contain, besides earth, gravel and stones, a variety of objects of great interest to the antiquarian, the ethnologist, and to science generally.

"Upwards of fifty kinds of baked earthenware utensils of all sizes and shapes, a considerable number of iron weapons and implements, chiefly knives or short sword-blades and hatchets, and a great quantity of bones and skulls were discovered. In one very interesting case, two small pots were found within a large one, together with the bones as in most cases of a nearly complete skeleton, containing what it was impossible to mistake for anything else but the outer coats of grains of rice and of the dry grain known in Tinnevelly as samei. The grain itself had disappeared, but the outer coating—probably of silica—had remained.

"Several places at considerable distances, one at least 300 or 400 yards from our principal excavation, were found to contain similar

---

* *Vide* Reports of the Archæological Survey, Southern Circle, for 1899-1900 to 1903-04, and of the Archæological Survey of India for 1902-03 and 1903-04.

† Proceedings of the Madras Government, Public Department (No. 329 of 27th March 1876).

sepulchral urns, and the surface of the quartz hill above was strewn over with broken pieces of pottery of a similar character. Our excavation in all probability only touched one point of an extensive ancient cemetery or catacomb in which the dead of an age, the habits of which are probably quite unknown in India at the present day, are disposed of in this singular manner, that is to say, by placing the skeleton or the body inside a large earthenware vase or pot together with two, three or four small pots apparently containing food for the dead and weapons and implements of iron ready for use when he reached another world." All these articles were taken away by Dr. Jagor for the Berlin Museum, and none of them reached the Madras Museum.*

At that time, the ground was used for the excavation of gravel, and as the workmen had a superstitious dread of disturbing the urns, which they have since got over, the exhumed urns, found in the course of the digging, were left standing or exposed. Thus a good collection of objects was found ready for removal without much trouble or expense.

A proposal was afterwards made to continue the excavations, by removing the whole of the soil from certain areas, leaving the urns standing exposed, which would have been rather a stupendous undertaking. But fortunately the proposal was dropped.

Orders were given by Government to leave the site undisturbed, but these appear to have been unattended to, for quarrying has been going on continuously ever since, with the result that vast quantities of these interesting relics must have been destroyed.

I first visited the site in the official year 1899–1900, when some digging was done. Further excavations were conducted by me for a few months annually up to the official year 1903–04. The collection now in the Madras Museum, and an almost equally large number of duplicates are the results obtained.

Description of the site.—The site extends to slightly over one hundred acres of land included in some villages at and near Ādichanallūr,† nearly twelve miles to the south-east of Tinnevelly town. It is a long piece of high ground, extending north to south, on the south bank of the river Tāmbaraparni, with a small hill at the end

* I have ascertained that certain objects collected by Dr. Jagor at Ādichanallūr are preserved in the Berlin Museum für Völkerkunde.

† Probably the village originally had the name of Ādittanallūr from the fact that one of the kings was known by the name of Ādittan.

adjoining the river. One peculiarity in regard to such prehistoric sites is that wherever possible, high land, waste or rocky or such as is unsuitable for cultivation, is that which has been generally selected for burial sites. This has already been mentioned in a previously published paper of mine.* Another fact is that in the neighbourhood of these sepulchral sites, there is often found the evidence of an ancient settlement. Cemeteries are usually situated on the south side of a town, the south being the abode of *Yama*, the God of Death; this having from time immemorial, been selected wherever possible, as the site for burials.

About the centre of the ground some three feet of surface soil is composed of gravel, with decomposed quartz rock below. The rock has been hollowed out for the urns, with a separate cavity for each of them.

In this burial ground the objects were found both inside and outside large urns of a pyriform shape. The urns were at an average distance of about six feet apart and at from three to twelve feet or more below the surface. Some were found placed over other ones. An idea of the deposits which exist in the whole area, may thus be obtained, as an acre probably holds over a thousand urns. This is the most extensive and important prehistoric burial place as yet known in Southern India. There are hundreds of prehistoric sites in several of the Madras districts which may contain two or three dozen urns, but none equal to this in extent.

Contents of the urns and description of the objects.—The objects found comprised gold,† bronze,‡ and iron § articles and pottery. The gold articles, which were probably used as diadems, vary in size and are oval in shape: some have a strip extending beyond the two extremities with a small hole for a wire or string at each end. They are thin plates ornamented with triangular and linear dotted designs

* "Some Prehistoric Burial Places in Southern India."—Journal of the Asiatic Society of Bengal, Vol. LVII, 1889.

† It might be interesting, on some future occasion, to get this analysed as considering the age, it is not likely to have any added alloy.

‡ From analysis it was found that the alloy consisted of copper 75 per cent., tin 23 per cent., lead 0·2 per cent., iron 0·4 per cent., and the casting seemed to contain some of the copper in the form of copper oxide.

§ On examination this was found to be a particularly pure wrought iron with a characteristic fibrous texture, with 25 per cent. carbon (by combustion).

and all were found folded up in a manner which suggests that some symbolical meaning may have been attached to the practice. Of iron, many implements and weapons were found, always placed point downwards, as if they had been thrust into the surrounding earth by the attendant mourners. There are no implements or weapons in bronze, all articles in this metal being vessels of varied shape, personal ornaments, such as rings, bangles and bracelets, or ornaments which have been attached to the bases and lids of vases, such as buffaloes with wide curved horns. The domestic animals represented in bronze are the buffalo, goat or sheep and cock; and the wild animals are the tiger, antelope and elephant. There are also representations of flying birds. There are sieves in bronze in the form of perforated cups fitted into small basins, the metal of these cups being extremely thin, and the basins only a little thicker. The perforations in the cup are in the form of dots arranged in a variety of designs, chiefly concentric circles around the bottom, and concentric semi-circles sometimes interlacing around the rim. Numerous human bones and skulls have been found, and one of the latter in particular, from an urn which was devoid of earth, retained its shape in perfect condition. This skull was taken from the bottom of the urn, which contained only bones of large size and the decomposed debris of smaller ones. Against one of the inner sides of the urn, leant the bones of the legs and arms of the skeleton, while below, in addition to the skull, were the vertebrae, ribs and other smaller bones exactly as one would expect them after the body, as evidently was the case in this instance, had been placed in the urn in a crouching or a sitting position. In only a few instances did an urn contain the complete bones of a skeleton, and in such cases it was always of large size, being nearly three feet in diameter.

Concerning the Ādichanallūr prehistoric burial site, M. Lapicque (Bull. Muséum d'Histoire Naturelle, 1905),* writes as follows:— "Avec une autorisation spéciale de l'administration anglaise, j'allai pratiquer quelques journées de fouilles dans le gisement réservé d'Adichanallour. J'ai rapporté un specimen des urnes funéraires, avec une collection assez complète du mobilier funéraire. . . . . J'ai rapporté aussi un crâne en assez bon état, et parfaitement déterminable. Il est hyperdolichocéphale et s' accorde avec la série que le service d' archéologie de Madras a déjà réunie. Je pense que la race d'Adichanallour appartient aux Protodravidiens."

* Annual Report of the Madras Government Museum, 1905-06, pp. 5 and 6.

Dr. Thurston states:—"The measurements of six of the most perfect skulls from Ādichanallūr in the Museum collection give the following results:—

Cephalic length, cm.	Cephalic breadth, cm.	Cephalic index.
18·8	12·4	66
19·1	12·7	66·5
18·3	12·4	67·8
18	12·2	67·8
18	12·8	71·1
16·8	13·1	78

Two of the skulls are conspicuously prognathous—a character which appears in a few Tamil and Telugu skulls in the Museum collection.

The following extract from my notes shows that the hyperdolichocephalic type survives in the dolichocephalic inhabitants of the Tamil country at the present day:—

Class.	Number examined.	Cephalic index below 70.
Palli	40	64·4; 66·9; 67; 68·9; 69·6.
Paraiyan	40	64·8; 69·2; 69·3; 69·5.
Vellāla	40	67·9; 69·6."

The modern system in India of interring a selection of bones from the cremated body seems to have been the method followed at Ādichanallūr, though there is no evidence of cremation at that place. All the finds, however, point to the fact that only certain bones were buried

On several of the bronzes are traces of cloth, which have been preserved by contact with the oxidized metal. Many of the vessels contained rice and millet seeds, while in a number of urns there were fragments of mica in pieces about an inch in length. The only stone implements found, were neolithic domestic utensils; a few cornelian beads, bronze beads and necklaces occurred also. A stone for grinding sandalwood was found buried outside, but all the other stone articles mentioned above were found inside urns. For the most part the pottery is well made, the clay being of a thin texture, in some cases red, in others black or a combination of the two colours. Only a few instances of applied colour occur, and little or no ornament is used; such as there is, consists of short dotted lines and is disposed diagonally around the rim. The urns are of coarse, thick, red pottery, adorned in some cases with incised crude ornament.

This site is still an inexhaustible field of archæological research of the most valuable description. The deposits, if fully excavated, would stock several museums with objects of the most interesting description, for almost every excavation brings to light something new. Many prehistoric sites have been examined in India, but none so extensive in its results as this. Large tracts at Ādichanallūr are yet untouched. The high ground on the east, within the limits of Ādichanallūr village, had anciently been a village site. In digging this ground, about a foot of deposited gravelly soil was found on the surface washed down from the higher ground. Below that, to a depth of about six feet, ashes mixed with the bones and horns of animals, broken pottery, etc., in short, the usual debris of a village site, were found.

From experience, it was possible to judge at the very commencement of the excavation of an urn, whether to expect a gold diadem in it or not, for generally the urns that contain diadems are at a great depth, and are overlaid with heavy stones. Out of many urns excavated, only a few gold ornaments were found, evidently in the case of persons of rank or importance. When the covering stones were removed, we first got a large supply of pottery, then several articles, such as weapons of iron, some of which have had wooden handles, and bronze vessels, lids or ornamental objects. These were in large numbers both inside and outside the urns.

The comparative rarity of bronze objects and their use for personal ornaments, show that this metal must have been scarce, highly valued, and used only by the higher class of people. Thus the people of those days appear to have been skilful in moulding pottery, in casting or working metals, in weaving and in working stone and wood. The ornamentation of the pottery consists only of embossed dots and incised lines, for the most part in triangular or simple geometrical designs. The bronzes exhibit a high degree of skill in workmanship and manipulation of the metal, while the same may be said of the iron implements. All this confirms historical accounts as to the early skill of Indians in the working of metals.

TINNEVELLY.

GOLD OBJECTS.

1 to 19. Diadems*—These are generally oval in shape and some have a strip prolonged at each extremity. In the ends of these strips are holes for a wire or string to fix the diadem to the forehead. Most of the diadems, however, have no strips at the ends and are simple ovals with a hole for the string pierced through each end. Some have linear and triangular ornaments made by dots impressed on the reverse, but six are unornamented. Pl. I, Figs. 15 to 20. Three of the smaller ones appear to be of inferior metal, gold plated. Pl. I, Figs. 18 to 20. The ovals vary in size from 2-3/16″ × 7/8″ to 6-5/8″ × 2-5/32″. There is another even smaller, which is simply a narrow strip 15/16″ in length by ¼″ broad.

In no. 1, two rows of raised dots in parallel lines run horizontally through the middle in continuation of the strips at both ends, and similar parallel lines branch off obliquely on both sides, resembling the ribs in leaves. In nos. 2 and 10, the dots, in the form of two parallel lines, run round the ends throughout; and three parallel lines run horizontally across the centre. The rest of the body is plain. In nos. 3 to 5, 7 and 11, the dots appear with no geometrical design. In no. 8, a single dotted line runs along the sides and across the centre with a leaf-like design in the middle. In no. 9 the dots are in a triangular design. In no. 12, a series of parallel lines runs throughout the body in a geometrical design. No. 13 is similar to nos. 2 and 10, but with dots throughout the body. No. 14 has the dots in an ornamental design, with three parallel lines running vertically through the centre.

20. Pear-shaped stone drop, plated with gold leaf (1″). Pl. I, Fig. 6.

* These are locally known as *Pattams* and the system of putting gold in some shape or other over the dead body is prevalent in orthodox Hindu homes even now-a-days. Dr. Marshall makes the following note on these objects (Annual Report of the Archæological Survey of India, 1902–03, Footnote on page 105):—"The gold frontlets are of thin gold leaf, so flimsy that they could not possibly have been used as jewellery in real life. They are mere imitations of the genuine article, substituted by the relations of the dead, who no doubt kept the more substantial jewellery for themselves. For similar instances of this economical piety towards the dead, see Frazer, *Pausanias*, Vol. III, page 107; Schliemann, *Mycenae*, page 156, etc.; E. Gardner, *New Chapters in Greek History*, page 343; E. B. Tylor, *Primitive Culture*, Vol. I, page 430."

BRONZE OBJECTS.

1. Bowl, imperfect, nearly one-half broken (H-3½″, D-4″).
2. Bowl with lines around the body and many lines between these. Rim broken on one side (H-2½″, D-4″).
3. Bowl, rim broken at one side (H-3″, D-4½″).
4. Bowl with a sieve cup attached (H-7″, D-5″). Body of the bowl and parts of the cup broken. The perforated holes in the sieve are indistinct through corrosion and earth attached. Pl. II, Fig. 1.
5. Round jar with cylindrical lid, almost perfect. It is of the same shape as another in pottery, no. 256. (H-7″, D-4″). Pl. II, Fig. 2.
6. Top of jar with cylindrical lid and bent rod ring handle, broken (H-4″, D-5″). Pl. II, Fig. 3.
7. Bowl with parallel lines running along the neck (H-2½″, D-4″).
8. Bowl, rim and upper part broken (H-3″, D-5″).
9. Bowl, with band around the centre filled with diagonal incised lines (H-2½″, D-4″).
10. Small jar without lid; a band around the neck. The bottom is highly polished in some parts.
11. Bowl with a series of raised parallel bands around it, and broken portions of lid attached. Inside is some white shale (H-2¾″, D-5½″).
12. Cup with a line around the rim (H-3″, D-4″). Highly polished in some parts and slightly broken on the top.
13. Sieve cup with wide bowl, much broken (H-3½″, D-8″). Perforations in sieve indistinctly visible.
14. Flat plate, broken (D-10″), with remains of a raised edge.
15. Disc with concentric circles above (D-7″). Probably used for frying cakes. (Fig. 13, page 129 of D.G.'s Annual, 1902-03.) Pl. II, Fig. 4.
16. Cylindrical lid with remains of large knob, broken (H-3″, D-6½″).
17. Bowl broken, similar to no. 3 (D-4½″, H-2½″).
18. Sieve cup attached to wide bowl, much broken (H-4″, D-8″).
19. Sieve cup with perforated holes in double semi-circular lines around the rim and parallel lines on the bottom, half broken (H-3″, D-3½″).
20. Bowl with a coating of earth inside. Slight traces of a dotted ornament on one side, broken in places at the rim (H-2½″, D-5″).
21. Portion of jar with three concentric raised bands around the neck (H-2″, D-3½″), much broken.

22. Jar filled with earth; bones and earth adhere to the outside (H-7", D-4").

23. Circular flat plate with incised concentric circles on the upper surface; projecting triangular handle (D-6"). (Fig. 12, page 129, D.G.'s Annual, 1902–03.) Pl. II, Fig. 5. Intended for frying cakes.

24. Mouth of a jar with a part of the body inside (H-2", D-3").

25. Fragmentary part of a large bowl (D-6").

26. Broken bowl with earth inside, bottom portion missing (H-2", D-5").

27. Sieve cup with semi-circular perforations surrounding the neck. Some parts of attached bowl remain. The bottom is broken (H-3", D-3½").

28. Ring stand attached to an earthen cup (H-1¼", D-2½").

29. Neck of a jar with the neck of a lid (H-2", D-3"); the body of the jar and top of the lid are missing.

30. Bowl with raised concentric bands around (H-2½", D-5½"). Broken in places.

31. Bowl with a moulded raised band below the neck, partly separated (H-3", D-5"). Body broken in parts.

32. Bowl with parallel moulded bands around the body. Incised ornaments between the bands (H-2½", D-4¾").

33. Top portion of a large pot with a bell mouth. The inside of the neck is highly polished and the rim at the bottom of the neck partly separated (M/D-4", D-9", H-5"). The body of the pot is missing. It resembles the more complete specimen no. 64.

34. Hollow plate, complete (D-5").

35. Wide shallow bowl much broken (D-8").

36. Small cup-shaped knob of a lid, broken. Similar to that which has been on no. 16 (H-2", D-3").

37. Sieve cup with well defined perforations (H-2", D-3½").

38. Cup with grooved parallel lines around, and diagonal incised lines between (H-1½", D-2½"). Bones and earth inside.

39. Part of a lid with a cup knob similar to nos. 16 and 36 (H-2", D-4").

40. Part of a bowl (H-4½", D-5½").

41. Part of neck, with the rim, of a pot (H-2½", D-6"). Raised parallel band around.

42. Neck of a jar with raised band at the bottom (H-1¼", D-4½").

43. Sieve cup (H-4¾", D-3"). Concentric perforations on bottom and semi-circles around.

44. Sieve cup much broken (H-2½", D-3").

45. Flat cylindrical lid of a jar (H-1", D-3").

46. Bowl with diagonal grooved lines at neck, nearly one-half broken (H-5", D-7").
47. Parts of a jar with band below the neck (H-7", D-5").
48. Wide bowl with broken sieve cup (H-5", D-6½").
49. Similar to no. 48, but larger (H-7", D-8½"). (Pl. 2, D.G's. Annual 1902–03.) Pl. II, Fig. 6.
50. Bowl similar to no. 46 (H-6", D-7½"). Very much disfigured in parts.
51. Jar with cylindrical lid in position, body much broken (H-6", D-4½").
52. Part of a bowl with grooved diagonal lines at the top, similar to no. 50 (H-6½", D-7").
53. Bowl with incised triangles around the body below the neck. Each alternate triangle is filled with diagonal incised lines (H-6", D-7"). (Fig. 7, page 125, D.G.'s Annual, 1902–03.) Pl. II, Fig. 7.
54. Part of a sieve cup with perforations in interlacing semi-circles (H-3", D-3").
55. Part of a lid with knob in the centre, surrounded by a circular band (D-6").
56. Top portion of a jar, body wanting. When complete it has been similar to no. 51 (H-4", D-3½").
57. Bowl, well polished in some places; with band around the neck and incised segments around the body, broken (H-4", D-5")
58. Jar with earth and bones adhering to the sides, much broken (H-4½", D-4").
59. *Kiṇṇam*, a peculiar shaped cup with concave sides: intended to hold oil and other liquids (H-3", D-4½"). Pl. II, Fig. 8.
60. Parts of the neck and body of a jar with rim attached (⊙ce, 7").
61. Jar without lid, slightly broken (H-5", D-3").
62. Jar with a broad band around the rim at neck (H-4", D-4"). (Fig. 9, page 126, D.G.'s Annual, 1902–03.) Pl. II, Fig. 9.
63. Cylindrical neck of a jar, body missing. Incised dots at one place on the neck (H-3", D-4").
64. *Kuḍam* (pot) with bell mouth, much broken (H-7", D-6", M/D 4½"). It is a more complete specimen of no. 33. Pl. II, Fig. 10.
65. Sieve cup with concentric semi-circular perforations (H-2", D-3");
66. Cup with turned spout for pouring out the contents; used for feeding infants. Modern ones with spouts are dissimilar in pattern (H-2", D-4". Length of spout 2".) Pl. II, Fig. 11.
67. Sieve cup, partly broken (H-3", D-3"). (Fig. 11, page 128, D.G.'s Annual, 1902–03.) Pl. II, Fig. 13.
68. *Kiṇṇam* differing from no. 59 in that the edges are elongated slightly broken. (H-2", D-3¾"). Pl. II, Fig. 12.
69. Cup (H-1½", D-3").

70. Cup slightly broken; when complete has been similar to no. 69 (H-1½″, D-3½″).

71. Upper part of a jar, with a high polish in parts: band with diagonal incised lines around (H-4″, D-5″).

72. *Kinnam* similar to no. 68 (H-2″, D-3½″).

73. Plate with sieve attached, much broken and with earth inside; has been similar to nos. 48 and 49 (H-4″, D-5½″).

74. Cup with incised triangular lines around the body (H-1½″ D-3½″). Pl. II, Fig. 14.

75. Small bowl with a raised band around the neck (H-3″, D-4″). Pl. II, Fig. 15.

76. Broken sieve cup (H-2¾″, D-3″).

77. Small broken cup, similar to nos. 68 and 72 (H-2″, D-3″).

78. Cylindrical neck of a jar, body missing (H-2¾″, D-4″).

79. Sieve cup with fragment of a lid and knob, broken (H-3″, D-3″).

80. Broken piece of a cup polished in parts, similar to no. 68 (⊙ce 6″).

81. Cylindrical neck of a jar with four bands around (H-2″, D-5″).

82. Polished cup with band of grooved crossed lines around the neck; metal very thin (H-1½″, D-4″).

83. Broken sieve cup (H-4″, D-3″).

84. Vase stand, with four rams having long twisted horns radiating from the centre of the base (H-6″, B-10″). On the backs of the animals are rods which bend inwards and upwards at an angle towards a ring. On the ring is a hollow plate or flat bowl. Vase stand, no. 91, is the only perfect example obtained, and shows what the missing parts of the others were like. The general arrangement seems to have been one of animals or rods resting on a circular base, with rods above them supporting a ring on which rests a bowl. There seems reason to believe, that these were used as stands for the large jars or bowls, which again were ornamented with the terminals, elsewhere described. Pl. II, Fig. 16.

85. Terminal having a central upright bar with globular bulbs on the top (H-4″, B-7″). Six bars curve upwards from the bottom and each of these branches into two at the top; they are each surmounted by a bulb. From above the centre of the central bar four other smaller bars curve upwards and each again is surmounted by a bulb. There are two principal classes of terminals. One has plain, moulded, pointed knobs, and the other has a vertical central column supporting an animal, while round it are numerous curved radiating rods surmounted by leaves, buds, or discs. A curious combination of the two is seen in no. 95. They were fixed on to the

cylindrical lids of certain kinds of bowls. Jar no. 6 has the cylindrical lid in position, with a ring top or handle for lifting it. (Fig. 6, page 12, Annual Report of A.D., 1902-03.) Pl. II, Fig. 17.

86. Terminal with twelve stems branching upward from the bottom in a curve, and each terminating in a circular disc or leaf having a semi-circular disc attached (H-5″, B-8″). A central upright stem is surmounted by these pointed leaves. Pl. II, Fig. 18.

87. Terminal of more elaborate form than no. 85. This example has twelve curved stems radiating from the bottom, and four curved stems higher up the central bar, each of which supports a bird. Pl. II, Fig. 19.

88. Terminal fragment, having five curved stems surmounted by pointed pear-shaped buds. About half of the stems and the central bar are missing (H-4″, B-8″). An animal which has been on the top of the central bar is apparently an elephant. A more complete example is seen in no. 92.

89. Terminal resembling a *kalayam*. A hollow bulbous body is surmounted by a pointed knob (H-6½″, D-6″). (Fig. 9, page 12, Annual Report of A.D., 1902–03.) Pl. II, Fig. 20.

90. Terminal, having a large under bulb, with five cocks facing inwards and resting on upright curved stems in different directions (H-4½″, B-10½″). (Fig. 4, page 12, Annual Report of A.D. 1902–03.) Pl. II, Fig. 21.

91. Vase stand with two tigers standing on the base (H-5″, B-6″). From the back of the body of each animal an upright bar supports a circular ring on which is the lower part of a flat bowl. (Fig. 12, page 13, Annual Report of A.D., 1902–03.) Pl. II, Fig. 22.

92. Terminal with traces of twelve stems all round, each ending in a pear-shaped bud (H-6½″, B-7½″). Only nine of the stems remain complete. Over the central bar is a buffalo with long curved horns. Pl. II, Fig. 23.

93. Terminal similar to the above, but with spherical buds on the extremities of the stems (H-5½″, B-7″). Pl. II, Fig. 24.

94. Large hollow bulb surmounted by a curved and pointed knob. From a ring at the base, curved rods radiate outwards. Each has terminated in a small knob. Only five of these remain (H-8″, D-3″). (Fig. 5, page 12, Annual Report of A.D., 1902–03.) Pl. II, Fig. 25.

95. Terminal with an elaborate series of bent and twisted rods radiating around. There are two series of such rods different from each other in form; those of the upper series are mostly in

position. They have been nine in all around a circular base. The rods of the lower series are loose (H-6″, B-1″). Pl. II, Fig. 33.

96. Antelope with one of the legs missing (H-4″, B-1½″). It has surmounted the central rod of a terminal. Pl. II, Fig. 26.

97. Cock (H-5″, B-2″). It has been fixed on the lid of a vase. It is of larger size, but similar to the cocks in no. 90. Pl. II, Fig. 27.

98 to 100. The first two are small terminal knobs resembling the tops of nos. 89 and 94 respectively. No. 100 is a fragment of a central rod of a terminal, with portions of the radiating rods remaining on its base (H-2″ to 4″, B-1″ to 2″).

101 to 104. Buffaloes with long curved horns (H-2″ to 3″, B-½″). Similar to those on nos. 92 and 93.

105. Dog with curled tail (H-2″, B-¼″). Pl. II, Fig. 28.

106 to 114. Bell ornaments for affixing to the anklets of dancers. No. 114 is of larger size than the others (H-1″ to 2″, B-½″ to ¾″). They are similar to those attached to no. 115. Pl. II, Fig. 29.

115. Anklet with five bells. It has been similarly used to those above noted. (3″), Pl. II, Fig. 31.

116. Terminal in the form of a conical base with circular disc and stem bearing four semi-circular discs. (H-5″, B-4″). Pl. II, Fig. 30.

117 and 118. Two small moulded pillars in the form of scent bottles; they may either have been used for this purpose or they may have surmounted a vase lid. On the under side of the base of no. 118 is a small piece of cloth oxidized by contact with the bronze. (H-5½″, 6″, B-½″, ¾″.)

119. Terminal with projecting and radiating straight and curved rods. (H-5″, B-8″). These have been ornamented with discs like those on no. 86. In the centre is a curved knob like that surmounting no 89.

120. A series of bangles of different sizes and thicknesses. They generally have a small knob at each end. Pl. II, Fig. 32.

121. A series of three styles or rods, and twelve rings; two of the latter are ½″ to ¾″ in diameter, and plated with gold; one has the setting for a stone, the others are plain; also an ear ornament or earthen *kammal* and five wire rings.

122. Three bronze necklaces consisting of thin wire rings which string together; two shell-necklaces from Korkai, and some detached stone beads; two pieces of green quartz, two pieces of red jasper, and agate and flint beads.

123. Fragments of bangles made of conch shell and other material, fish vertebræ and a shell (from Korkai).

IRON OBJECTS.

1\. Implement, solid and flat for three-fourths of its length (L-1′ 2″). Slightly sharpened at the end; the base is hollow and broad, intended to hold a wooden shaft. Pl. III, Fig. 1.

2\. Solid bar, rectangular in section and tapering to a sharp point (L-2′ 8″, B-½″). Pl. III, Fig. 2.

3 to 7. Spear heads of various form (L-1′ 7″ to 1′ 5″, B. of blade ¾″ to 2″). The ends are hollow for fixing to a wooden shaft. Nos. 3, 4 and 7 have blades with straight edges tapering to a point. Nos. 5 and 6 have blades with curved edges broadest in the centre. For nos. 3, 4 and 5, see Pl. III, Figs. 3 to 5.

8 to 20. Flat chisels (L-6″ to 4″, B-1″ to ½″). Nos. 8 to 17 are broad at the edge and taper to a point. For nos. 15, 17, 18, see Pl. III, Figs. 6 to 8.)

21\. *Trisūlam* (Trident). L-3′ 2″, B. of top portion 7¼″ and ⊙ce of shaft 2″). The handle is 2″ long, square in section with a pointed knob at the end. The three prongs are flat in section, tapering to points; the outer prongs form a semi-circular curve at the base across which is a cross-bar. (Fig. 17, page 134 of D.G.'s Annual, 1902-03.) Pl. III, Fig. 22.

22\. Spear (L-2′ 4″, of blade 2″). The two sides are concave with sharp edges; the blade gradually tapers to the point; the base is hollow for fixing a wooden shaft and is 4″ in length. Pl. III, Fig. 10.

23 to 28. Double-edged swords (L-2′ to 1′ 9″, B. of blade 2″ to 1½″). Except no. 25 which has a slight taper to the point, the sides of the others are parallel, with a sharp angular point; the handle is a pointed spike, on to which would be fitted a wooden handle.

29 to 41. Barbed javelins (L-7½″ to 6″, B. of blade 1″ to ¾″). The blades are curved convexly, and have hollow butts. For no. 30, see Pl. III, Fig. 9.

42\. A curious weapon (L-5½″, B-1″) formed like a lance, but neither the blade sides nor the tip are sharp as in the majority of the finds.

43 to 46. Lances (L-6″ to 5″, B. of blade ½″ to ¼″). The body is very narrow having only a width of about ½″; a hollow tube forms the butt end. For no. 44, see Pl. III, Fig. 17.

47\. Small dagger (L-7″, B. of blade 2″). Broken in the middle; the sides of the blade are parallel and taper to the point. The spike at the hilt is imperfect.

48 to 51. Lances (L-1′ 9″ to 1′ 2½″, B. of blade 2″ to 2¼″). No. 48 has a broad blade of 1½″, having the sides nearly parallel for the

most of its length and a tapering point. The butt end of the blade is cut straight across; the butt is tubular. Nos. 49 to 51 have narrow tapering blades and round hollow butts. For nos. 48 and 49, see Pl. III, Figs. 11 and 12.

52 to **54.** Small lances (L-7″ to 6″, B. of blade 1″ to ¾″) with curved convex blades and hollow butts. The pointed top in no. 52 is broken.

55. Lance with blade rectangular in section, tapering to a point; hollow tube butt (L-6″, B-¼″).

56 and **57.** Lances with narrow blades (L-5½″, 5″; B-⅓″ to ¼″). No. 56 is broken.

58 to **60.** Barbed arrow-heads (L-5″ to 1½″, B-½″ to 1¼″). No. 60 is peculiarly broad in the blade. Pl. III, Fig. 13.

61 and **62.** Daggers (L-9″, 6″; B. of blade 1″ to ¾″) with spiked handles; the blades gradually taper to the point; the tip is bent in the former, and broken in the latter.

63. Lance with tapering blade and hollow butt; the latter is slightly broken (L-8½″, B-¾″).

64. Rod (L-6½″, ⊙ᶜᵉ 1″) much corroded, with pieces of quartz and gravel adhering to it.

65. Hollow tube handle of lance similar to no. 55 (H-5″, ⊙ᶜᵉ ¾″).

66 to **68.** Javelins (L-6″ to 4½″, B. of blade ¾″ to 1″). Similar to nos. 29 to 41, but the barbs are missing.

69. Lance (L-7½″, B-¾″) similar to no. 63. Fragments of quartz adhere to it.

70. Dagger with tapering point. (L-10½″, B-1″). There is a ring at the hilt for fixing a wooden handle.

71 to **73.** Daggers (L-1′ to 10″, B-1¼″ to 1½″). Tapering sides in no. 71, angular point in no. 73, the point in no. 71 is broken; they have spiked hilts.

74. Hatchet (L-6″, B-2″) broadest at the cutting edge. The diagonal ring found on other examples for fixing the wooden handle is missing.

75 to **80.** Chisels with long triangular haft (L-7½″ to 9½″, B. of blade at middle 1″ to 3″). The pointed spiked portion is probably intended for the wooden handle. For no. 79, see Pl. III, Fig. 14. (Fig. 12, Plate III, Annual Report of A.D., 1903-04).

81. Double-edged sword with parallel sides and angular point (L-2′ 8″, B-2¾″). The hilt is pick-shaped with iron rivets to fix the wooden handle. (Plate IV, Annual Report of A.D., 1903.) Pl. III, Fig. 16.

82. Lance with long round hollow shaft; nearly one-half of the upper blade is broken. (L-1′, B. of blade 1″, ⊙ce of shaft 2″.)

83 to **86.** Hollow iron handles with rods through the centre (L-$5\frac{1}{2}$″ to $8\frac{1}{2}$″, ⊙ce 3″ to 4″). These have knobs on the top and are pointed; probably they were intended to drill wood by means of string wrapped around the handles, drawn backwards and forwards, as is done by Indian carpenters at the present day. For no. 84, see Pl. III, Fig. 15.

87. Lance with hollow handle (L-$6\frac{1}{2}$″, B. of blade $\frac{3}{4}$″). The top portion of the blade is broken.

88 to **96.** Swords with various curved blades tapering to a point (L-1′ $7\frac{1}{2}$″ to 2′ 2″, B-$1\frac{3}{4}$″ to 2″). No. 88 has a curious round flat handle, and several have raised rims along half the middle of the blade. For no. 88, see Pl. III, Fig. 18. All are double-edged and have spiked hilts, except no. 94 which is a modification of no. 81. Nos. 91 and 96 are bent in the middle, on account of the uneven weight which has rested on them after being placed in the urns at the time of burial. Nos. 90 and 95 are peculiar in that the blade is broad near the hilt and point, and concave edged at the middle.

97. Tripod with curved legs (D. of the circular ring on the top $9\frac{1}{2}$″, H-7″, bent leg $7\frac{1}{2}$″). This is a perfect specimen. (Fig. 21, page 14, Annual Report of A.D., 1902-03.) Pl. III, Fig. 26.

98 to **102.** Lances with tapering blades and hollow handles (L-1′ $6\frac{1}{2}$″ to 2′ 11″, B. of blade $2\frac{1}{4}$″ to $2\frac{1}{2}$″.) In nos. 98 and 102 the handles are imperfect. For no, 101, see Pl. III, Fig. 19.

103 to **106.** Swords (L-2′ 10″ to 2′, B-$1\frac{3}{4}$″ to 2″). No. 104 is slightly bent. Nos. 103 and 106 have sharp raised rims running up the centre of half the blade, and tapering points. Nos 104 and 105 have hilts resembling nos. 81 and 94, and angular points.

107. Miscellaneous small objects consisting of bangles, rods, a bar with broad handle at each end, a bell, nails, a small cylindrical box, and other small articles numbering in all thirty-one. Pl. IV, Fig. 1.

108. A curious article resembling a broad trident, with two curved, sharpened, tapering blades and a central point above a broad bottom plate. This latter is perforated with fine curved lines, and through the bottom bar are six holes probably intended for nails rivetted to the object to which this was fixed. This appears to have been a weapon of some kind, but its purpose is not certain. One of the curved blades is broken. (Fig. 14, page 13, Annual Report of A.D., 1902–03.) Pl. III, Fig. 24. (L-1′ 1″, B-7″.)

109 and 110. Hooks with two curved rods on each side of a central rod (L-5½", 7"; B-1", 5½"). These have formed the bent rods fixed across the upper ends of *śūlams* such as those on nos. 362 to 365, and others of the class in the same case. For no. 110 see Pl. III, Fig. 25.

111 to 115. Knives (L-1' to 1' 3", B-1¼" to 1¾"); similar to those used now-a-days for cutting leaves and fruit. The blade is convex on each side, tapering to a point, and the hilt ends in a circular ring, with a hole in the centre of nos. 113 to 115. (Fig. 16, page 14, Annual Report of A.D., 1902-03.) For nos. 111, 112 and 115, see Pl. III, Figs. 20, 21 and 23.

116 to 127. Daggers (L-1' to 8½", B-1¾" to 2"). Nos. 116 to 120 have a spiked handle with a ring at the hilt. For no. 120, Pl. IV, Fig. 2. Nos. 121 to 127 have a spiked handle without rings, except no. 123 which has concave sides; the others have parallel-sided blades with an angular point.

128. A fine specimen of a sacrificial sword (L-4', B-3".) The blade is double-edged, with a raised central rim along the greater part of the middle of the blade on both sides. The sides are concave-edged for the lower part of the length, convex above, tapering to a point. The bottom part of the hilt is slightly broken. Pl. V, Fig. 1.

129. A curious article (L-1' 2½", H-4") which resembles no. 108 and has doubtless been used for the same purpose. The top plate is slightly curved on both the sides, and in the bottom plate are holes intended probably for rivetting nails to the body of the object or handle. Pl. IV, Fig. 4.

130. Chisel (L-4", B-¾"). The butt is slightly broken.

131 to 145. Lances with hollow butts and tapering blades. (L-6", B. of blade ¼" to 1"); nos. 143 and 144 have the hollow tube butts slightly broken. No. 145 has fragments of quartz adhering to it.

146 to 151. Javelins (L-6" to 7", B-¾" to 1"); nos. 146 and 148 are coated with lime, and the barbs in all are more or less broken. For no. 149, see Pl. IV, Fig. 5.

152. Arrowhead (L-4", B-1"). Pl. IV, Fig. 6.

153 to 165. Daggers with tapering blades and spiked handles (L-9½" to 11½", B-1½" to 3¼"). In nos. 154 to 162 the handle is slightly broken; nos. 163 and 165 have the tips in imperfect condition. For no. 153, see Pl. IV, Fig. 7.

166 to 169. Reaping hooks or curved knives of various forms. (L-1' 2½" to 6", B. of blade 2" to ½"). These have curved blades with a straight spiked hilt for affixing to the wooden handle.

(Fig. 15, page 14 of Annual Report of A.D., 1902-03.) For nos. 167 and 168, see Pl. IV, Figs. 8 and 10.

170 to **181.** Javelins (L-6″ to 5″, B-1¼″ to 1″). In some of these, the curved barbs at the bottom are broken. Nos. 177 and 179 have fragments of quartz attached to the metal.

182 to **213.** *Mammuṭṭis* or spades (L-1′ 2″×4½″ to 6″ × 2½″). Though different from the modern Indian spade they have been used for the same purpose, namely for digging earth. They are generally similar in shape, though varying in size and other details and are made of thick, flat metal, with a round projection or flange on each edge of the butt-end, bent inwards to form a hold for the handle, which was placed at right angles to the blade. They are broadest at the digging end. There are two distinct forms, some being short and of medium size with sides variously curved, while others have long straight sides. Modern ones resemble in some respects the latter pattern, except that there are no side flanges and only a central haft or ring for the handle. (Figs. 18 to 21, page 137 of D.G.'s Annual, 1902-03.) For nos. 182, 187, 189, 201, 204, 211, see Pl. IV, Figs. 3, 11, 12, 13, 14, 15 respectively.

214 to **221.** Hatchets (7″ × 3″ to 5½″ × 2″). These consist of a thick plate of flat metal with straight sides; the cutting edge is rounded with a breadth greater than the butt. (Fig. 22, page 14, Annual Report of A.D., 1902-03.) For no. 214, see Pl. IV, Fig. 16.

222 to **226.** Axes (8½″ × 3″ to 8″ × 2½″). These are of a class similar to nos. 214 to 221, but slightly larger, with diagonal detached rings across the butt-ends for affixing to a split wooden handle. Others similar have been found at some of the excavations at Buddhist sites in the north-east of the Presidency, notably at Rāmatīrtham. For no. 223, see Pl. IV, Fig. 17.

227. *Triśūlam* (Trident) (L-3′ 3″, shaft 2′ 2″, B. of top 3¾″). The handle is rectangular in section and has a round knob at the end. There is no cross-bar at the base of the prongs, as in the other already described (no. 21, Pl. III, Fig. 22). One side prong is completely broken and the middle one slightly so.

228 to **234.** Chisels of angular form (L-5″ to 3″, B-1″ to ¾″). No. 232 is broken in the middle and is in two pieces. No. 234 is thickly encrusted with earth. For nos. 228 and 231, see Pl. IV, Figs. 18 and 19.

235 and **236.** Axes (6″ × 2½″). They have detached rings near the butt-end. For no. 235, see Pl. IV, Fig. 20.

237 to 251. Double-edged swords with spiked hilts (L-2′ 6″ to 1′ 4″, B-1$\frac{3}{4}$″ to 2$\frac{3}{4}$″). Except nos. 241 and 248 to 251, all have parallel sides and angular or curved points. Nos. 241 to 248 have a raised rim along the centre of the blade. No. 241 has a double curve on the sides, concave near the hilt and convex above the centre, tapering to the point. No. 238 has nails in the hilt for fixing the wooden handle. In no. 242 the blade is bent in a double curve, the result of pressure in the urn. No. 244 has the hilt bent at right angles. For nos. 237, 238, 240, see Pl. V, Figs. 2 to 4.

252 to 259. Lances (L-1′ 8″ to 1′, B. of blade 1$\frac{1}{4}$″ to 2$\frac{1}{4}$″). They have, hollow tube handles, greatly varying in the proportion they bear to the blade. No. 255 is encrusted with gravel. For no. 252, See Pl. V, Fig. 13.

260 to 268. Hanging saucer-lamps (4″ diameter). These had originally arched bars on two sides of the saucer, with hanging rods and chains to suspend them. No. 266 is complete (H-8″) but the rest have only the saucer remaining, in which fragments of the upper parts are placed. A piece of the suspending chain is placed in nos. 260 and 265. No. 268 has part of the arched side remaining.

269 and 270. Lances with hollow tube handles (L-1′ 5″ and 1′ 2″, B. of blade 1″ and $\frac{3}{4}$″).

271 to 282. Rods (L-1′ 2″ to 1′ 8″, $\odot^{ce}$ at middle 2″ to 3″). These are rounded with an elongated oval bulge in the middle and a knob at each end. They resemble the beams of weighing scales, but the exact purposes for which they were intended cannot be definitely stated.

283 to 286. Javelins with hollow tube butts. Only parts of the barbs remain. (L-6″ to 5″, B-1″ to $\frac{3}{4}$″).

287 to 294. Lances with hollow tube handles. (L-6$\frac{1}{2}$″ to 4″, B-$\frac{1}{2}$″ to $\frac{1}{4}$″). Nos. 287, 290, 293, are encrusted with earth. For no. 287, see Pl. IV, Fig. 22.

295. Dagger of peculiar shape (L-6″, B-2$\frac{1}{2}$″). The blade is about 2″ wide at the upper part and narrower at the lower end. The hilt is missing. Pl. IV, Fig. 23.

296. Chisel of peculiar shape (L-9″, B-$\frac{1}{2}$″). The blade has parallel sides and is broken at the top. It has a spiked hilt which is much longer than the blade. Pl. IV, Fig. 24.

297 and 298. Hatchets (5$\frac{1}{2}$″ × 2$\frac{1}{2}$″ to 4$\frac{1}{2}$″ × 2$\frac{1}{4}$″). These are broad in proportion to the length. They have no detached ring at the butt-end.

299 to **302.** Lances (L-7″ to 7½″, B-¾″ to 1″). The hollow tube handles are broken in all. Nos. 299 and 302 are thickly encrusted with gravel; the former has been barbed.

303 to **305.** Angular chisels tapering to a point at the butt-end (L-4″ to 3¾″, B. of middle blade ¼″ to ½″.)

306. Thick plate of iron measuring 1′ 10″ × 3½″. The sides are parallel and the ends rounded. One end is sharp and the other is blunt as if it had been hammered; it has probably been used for splitting logs of wood. Pl. V, Fig. 6.

307 to **310.** Double-edged swords (L-2′ 3½″ to 1′ 10″, B-1¾″ to 2¼″). Nos. 307 and 308 have curved sides to the blades, with raised rims along the lower part of the middle of the blade. Nos. 309 and 310 have parallel sides and angular points of 2″ width.

311 and **312.** Axes (9½″ × 3″, 9″ × 2″). They have detached rings on the butt-end.

313 and **314.** Hatchets (7½″ × 2″, 7″ × 1¾″). These have no rings.

315 to **318.** Daggers (L-1′ 1″ to 9″, B-1¼″ to 2″). These have spiked hilts for wooden handles.

319 to **321.** Lances with solid butts (L-8″ to 7½″, B-1″ to ½″). For no. 321, see Pl. IV, Fig. 25.

322 to **333.** Rods (L-1′ 7″ to 9″, ⊙ce at middle 2″ to 3″). These are of a similar class to nos. 271 to 282. For no. 326, Pl. V, Fig. 14.

334 to **339.** Javelins with hollow butts (L-6″ to 5½″, B-1½″ to 1″).

340 to **348.** Lances with hollow tube handles (L-6″ to 5″, B-1″ to ¾″).

349. Sword (L-1′ 10″, B-2¾″). It has a spiked handle and parallel-sided blade. It is much bent in the middle due to pressure while in the urn. Pl. V, Fig. 15.

350 to **359.** Saucer-lamps (D. of pan 4¼″ to 3¼″, H-6¼″ to 6″). Some have circular arched bars, *e.g.*, nos. 354 and 358, and the latter has a rod through the top for hanging by a chain. No. 355 has two upright bars and a top cross rod with part of the hanging rod remaining. No. 356 has had the same kind of arched bars, but they are broken off. Nos. 353 and 357 have the hanging rod fixed in the centre of the saucer; fragments are placed in nos. 351, 356 and 359. (Figs 23 and 24, page 138 of D.G.'s Annual, 1902-03.) For nos. 353, 355, 358, see Pl. V, Figs. 11, 8 and 9 respectively.

360. Lance with hollow tube butt (L-1′ 2″, B. of blade 1¾″).

361. Knife (L-1′ 4½″, B-2″). The hilt is flat and circular, with a hole through the centre.

362 to 365. *Śūlams* (L-3′ 2″ to 2′ 3″, B. of blade ½″ to 1″). These have cross-pieces with bent arms at the top of the shaft only. The shafts are square in section, and have a knob at the end, and generally the lower part is cut in screw form. For nos. 362, 365, see Pl. V, Figs. 5 and 7.

366 and 367. Saucer-lamps (D-5½″ and 4½″). The side beams are wanting. Some fragments are placed in no. 366.

368. Curved knife with bent spiked handle (L-7″, B-¾″). Some gravel adheres to it. Pl. IV, Fig. 9.

369. Sword (L-2′ 2″, B-2½″). This is bent almost double in the middle of the blade which is 3″ in width. It has parallel sides, angular point and hilt studded with rivets like no. 81. The bend is due to pressure in the urn. Pl. V, Fig. 10.

370 to 374. *Śūlams* (L-3′ 7″ to 2′ 11″, B-¾″ to 1″). These are similar to nos. 362 to 365. In no. 372, the cross bars are missing.

375 to 377. Swords (L-2′ 4″ to 2′, B-2″ to 2½″). These have spiked shaped handles; the blade is about 2″ in width.

378. *Mammuṭṭi* or spade (5¼″ × 2″).

379. Saucer-lamp (D-3″).

380 to 383. *Śūlams* (L-3′ 1½″ to 2′ 4″, B-½″ to ¾″). Similar to others. No. 380 has the whole length of the shaft square in section. Some of the cross bars are missing.

384. Sword (L-1′ 6″, B-½″.) This has a raised rim right up the centre of the blade. The blade is completely bent at the middle. Pl. IV, Fig. 21.

385 to 394. Iron pendants (L-1′ 10″ to 1′ 1″, B-2′ 5″ to 10″). These may have been used for suspending saucer-lamps. They have a strong broad suspending ring at the top of a vertical rod of square section, which again has large hooks of different design at the bottom, varying in number from two to four. Close to the top suspending ring, a series of from four to eight long arms or ribs radiate outwards and downwards, resembling in this respect the ribs of an ordinary umbrella and terminate in hooks of thin flat metal. All are exhibited over Pottery Cases. For no. 386, see Pl. V, Fig. 12. (Fig. 22, page 138 of D.G.'s Annual, 1902–03.)

POTTERY.

[All the objects numbered 1 to 36 have ring-stands for support, and the measurements given against each are the diameter of the mouth of the vessel and depth. The ring-stands are circular, concave in the middle and black-polished; they are all generally of one form and the variations which occur, are chiefly in size.]

1. Bowl with red body and black around the rim (M/D-7″, H-1½″).

2. *Kiṇṇam** with beaded rim, having three parallel grooved lines around the top of the body and below the rim (M/D-6″, H-3″). Pl. VI, Fig. 2.

3. *Śaṭṭi* (M/D-7″, H-4″). Polished black inside and red outside, with traces of black around rim.

4. *Kiṇṇam* (M/D-7″, H-3½″). With a line running over the body just below the rim, the latter slightly broken. Colour red outside and black inside, covered with a red deposit.

5. *Kuṇḍu Bōgiṇi* (M/D-5″, H-4½″). Inside black; outside polished black on the upper half and red on the bottom.

6. *Śaṭṭi* (M/D-6½″, H-3″). With a wide mouth and flat conical bottom. Black inside. Polished black outside around the rim, and bottom red. Pl. VI, Fig. 3.

7. *Kuṇḍu Bōgiṇi* (M/D-5″, H-3¾″) with original earth inside in which another smaller vessel is embedded. Colour on outside black, around the rim with red bottom. Pl VI, Fig. 4.

8. *Śaṭṭi* (M/D-7″, H-3½″). Inside black, outside polished black and red.† Pl. VI, Fig. 5.

9. Bowl with flat conical bottom. Inside black, outside black and red. Filled with bones.

10 and 11. *Kiṇṇam* with rim and line running around the body below. Red, but show traces of black polish inside and out (M/D-6″, H-3½″ each). For no. 10, see Pl. VI, Fig. 6.

12. *Śaruvaśaṭṭi* (M/D-6½″, H-3″) with rim; red but shows traces of having been coloured black on upper part; some original earth inside. Pl. VI, Fig. 7.

13 *Mūḍi* (M/D-7″, H-2½″). Cover of a pot. Another of the same kind is fixed inside. Colour red with black rim. Pl. VI, Fig. 8.

14. *Kuṇḍu Bōgiṇi* (M/D-5″, H-3″) with portions of a *mūḍi* over it The top portion is broken. Earth and some bones inside. Black and red. Pl. VI, Fig. 9.

15. *Kuṇḍu Bōgiṇi* (M/D-5″, H-3″). An incised line runs around below the rim. Black and red.

16 to 18. *Mūḍis* (M/D-7½″ to 7″, H-3″ to 2½″). In no. 17 there are some bones. An incised line around the rim of no. 18. Black and red.

---

* The names given to the various vessels are those by which similarly shaped articles are now known in the local Tamil dialect; but it should be understood that in the other Tamil districts, and in the Kanarese and Telugu country, a variety of different names is applied to the same objects. The shape of any one kind may vary. All are generally used for cooking or storing viands. Photographs of the most typical of each kind will be found among the plates.

† When the words "black and red" are used, it indicates that polished black extends around the rim, with a red bottom. The material itself is usually red, and the black is a surface polish.

19. *Śinna Kuṇḍu Bōgiṇi* (M/D-$3\frac{1}{2}$″, H-$2\frac{1}{2}$″). Black and red. Pl. VI, Fig. 10.

20. *Mūḍi* (M/D-7″, H-$2\frac{1}{2}$″). Rim broken. Black and red outside inside black.

21. *Kuṇḍān* (M/D-7″, H-$3\frac{1}{2}$″). Black and red outside; black, but stained with red earth inside. Pl. VI, Fig. 11.

22 and 23. *Śaṭṭis*, with flat conical base. Black and red outside; inside black (M/D-$7\frac{1}{2}$″ to 6″, H-$3\frac{1}{2}$″ to $2\frac{1}{2}$″.) Pl. VI, Fig. 12.

24. *Kiṇṇam* (M/D-5″, H-3″). A pair of incised lines around below the rim. Black and red outside, black inside. Pl. VI, Fig. 13.

25 to 27. *Mūḍis* (M/D-8″ to 7″, H-$3\frac{1}{2}$″ to 3″). There are some bones in no. 26. Black and red outside; black inside. For no. 26, see Pl. VI, Fig. 14.

28 to 35. *Śaṭṭis*, (M/D-5″ to $5\frac{1}{2}$″, H-$2\frac{1}{2}$″ to 3″). Black and red outside; black inside. The ring-stand under no. 33 goes by the name of *kumbā*, in which one of the counterparts varies from the other, the upper part being cupshaped. For no. 33, see Pl. VI, Fig. 15.

36. *Śaṭṭi* (M/D-7″, H-$2\frac{1}{2}$″). A *mūḍi* is attached, with earth inside. Red and black. Pl. VI, Fig. 16.

NOTE.—Each of the objects numbered 37 to 86 is placed on a ring-stand, except no. 79 which itself is a ring-stand.

37 and 38. *Kalayams* (M/D-4″ each, H-$4\frac{1}{4}$″ and 4″). Rims slightly broken. Black and red outside; black inside. Pl. VI, Fig. 17.

39. Bowl with conical base. Black and red outside; inside black (M/D-6″, H-$3\frac{1}{4}$″).

40. *Mūsai* (M/D-5″, H-4″). Two parallel grooved lines around the body. Black and red outside; black inside. Pl. VI, Fig. 18.

41. *Bōgiṇi* (M/D-7″, H-5″). Bottom slightly pointed. Black and red outside; inside black. Pl. VI, Fig. 19.

42. *Kuṇḍu Bōgiṇi* (M/D-5″, H-$4\frac{3}{4}$″. ⊙ce at m.b. 1′8″). Black and red outside; inside black. Pl. VI, Fig. 20.

43. *Maravai* (M/D-5″, H-4″). Has a flat bottom. Black and red outside; black inside. Pl. VI, Fig. 32.

44 and 45. *Śiṇṇa Kuṇḍān*. Outside black and red; inside black. (M/D-$4\frac{3}{4}$″ to $4\frac{1}{4}$″, H-4″ to 3″. ⊙ce at m.b. 10″).

46. *Śiṇṇa Kalayam* (M/D-2″, H-$2\frac{1}{2}$″). Is full of earth. Black and red outside. Elongated ring-stand. Pl. VI, Fig. 21.

47. *Mūḍi* (M/D-$4\frac{1}{2}$″, H-3″). Black and red outside; black inside.

48. *Śombu* (M/D-$2\frac{1}{2}$″, H-$3\frac{1}{2}$″, ⊙ce at m.b. 1′). Black and red outside; black inside. Pl. VI, Fig. 22.

49. *Kuṇḍān* (M/D-5", H-4"). Black and red outside; inside black.

50. *Kuṇḍu Bōgiṇi* (M/D-$3\frac{1}{2}$", H-$4\frac{1}{4}$"; $\odot^{ce}$ of the body 1' 4"). Black and red outside; inside black.

51. *Kuṇḍān* (M/D-$5\frac{1}{4}$", H-4"). Lines around, below the rim. Inside black; outside red.

52. *Peria Mūsai* (M/D-$4\frac{1}{4}$", H-$6\frac{1}{2}$"). Rim broken. Black and red outside; inside black.

53. *Kuṇḍān* (M/D-$4\frac{1}{2}$", H-$3\frac{1}{2}$"). Black and red outside; inside black.

54. *Mūḍi* (M/D-$4\frac{1}{2}$", H-$2\frac{1}{4}$"). Slight breakage on the rim. Black and red outside; inside black.

55. *Śithai Kuṇḍān* (M/D-2", H-4". $\odot^{ce}$ at m.b. 1' $7\frac{3}{4}$"). Globular, slightly elongated at bottom; narrow mouth. Black throughout. Pl. VI, Fig. 23.

56. *Kuṇḍu Śombu* (M/D-3", H-$4\frac{3}{4}$". $\odot^{ce}$ 1' 1"). Black and red outside; black inside.

57. *Mūḍi* (M/D-$4\frac{1}{2}$", H-4"). Black and red outside; black inside.

58. *Kiṇṇam* (M/D-$4\frac{3}{4}$", H-3"). Black and red outside; black inside.

59. *Jāḍi* (M/D-3", H-$3\frac{3}{4}$", $\odot^{ce}$ at m.b. 1' 1"). Elongated conical bottom. Black and red outside; black inside. Pl. VI, Fig. 24.

60. *Śombu* (M/D-2", H-$3\frac{1}{2}$", $\odot^{ce}$ at m.b. 1'). Red with traces of black on neck.

61. *Kalayam* (M/D-$2\frac{1}{4}$", H-$2\frac{1}{2}$"). Red throughout.

62. *Bōgiṇi* (M/D-$4\frac{3}{4}$", H-5"). Black and red outside; black inside.

63. *Pallāi* (M/D-$2\frac{3}{4}$", H-$1\frac{1}{4}$"). Black and red outside, black inside Pl. VI, Fig. 25.

64 and 65. *Uruḷi* (M/D-$3\frac{1}{2}$" to 4", H-2" to $2\frac{1}{2}$"). Black and red outside; black inside. For no. 64, see Pl. VI, Fig. 26.

66. *Jāḍi* (M/D-$2\frac{1}{2}$", H-2", $\odot^{ce}$-1'). Slightly pointed bottom. Black and red outside; black inside.

67. *Kalayam* (M/D-$2\frac{1}{2}$", H-2", $\odot^{ce}$ at m.b. 10"). Black and red outside; inside black.

68 and 69. *Mūḍis* (M/D-$3\frac{1}{2}$" and 3", H-$2\frac{3}{4}$" and $2\frac{1}{2}$"). No. 69 is full of earth.

Black and red outside; inside black. For no. 68, see Pl. VI, Fig. 27.

70. *Kalayam* (M/D-3", H-3", $\odot^{ce}$ at m.b. 1' $1\frac{1}{2}$".) Filled with earth; black and red outside.

71. *Uruḷi* (M/D-4", H-3", $\odot^{ce}$ at m.b. 1' 4"). Sharp convex side. Black and red outside; inside black. Pl. VI, Fig. 28.

72 and 73. *Kuḍuvai* (M/D-$2\frac{1}{2}$" and $2\frac{1}{4}$", H-3" and $2\frac{3}{4}$", $\odot^{ce}$ 11" and 1'). Black and red outside; inside black. Pl. VI, Fig. 29.

74 to 76. *Kiṇṇam* (M/D-3" to $3\frac{1}{4}$", H-$2\frac{1}{4}$" to $2\frac{1}{2}$"). Nos. 74 and 76 are entirely black. No. 75 is black and red outside and black inside.

77. *Kuḍuvai* (M/D-2½″, H-3″, ⊙^{ce} 11″). Black and red outside, black inside.

78. *Kuṇḍu Bōgiṇi* (M/D-3¾″, H-3″). Black and red outside; inside black.

79. Ring-stand (M/D-3¾″, H-3½″, ⊙^{ce} at m.b. 5½″). Elongated cup-shaped top. Black.

80. *Uruḷi* (M/D-5½″, H-2½″). Black and red outside ; black inside.

81 and 82. *Kalayam* (M/D-2″ and 1½″, H-2½″ and 3″, ⊙^{ce} 9½″ and 9¼″). No. 81 is red, no. 82 black and red outside, black inside. Pl. VI, Fig. 30 for no. 81.

83. *Mūḍi* (M/D-3½″, H-2½″). Black and red outside ; black inside.

84. *Kuḍuvai* (M/D-2½″, H-3¼″, ⊙^{ce} 1′). Black and red outside ; inside black.

85. *Maravai* (M/D-2″, H-2¼″). Black and red outside ; inside black. Pl. VI, Fig. 31.

86. *Kalayam* (M/D-2″, H-1¾″, ⊙^{ce} 10″). Black and red outside ; inside black.

87. *Mūsai* (M/D-4½″, H-4½″). Some bones are inside. There is a black ring-stand below.

88. *Mūḍi* (M/D-3½″, H-2½″). Below is a black ring-stand covered with a red deposit.

89. *Kuṇḍān* (M/D-4″, H-3″). Red coloured throughout.

90. *Śombu* (M/D-2½″, H-3¼″, ⊙^{ce} at m.b. 1′ 1″).

91. *Pallāi* (M/D-4″, H-4¼″, ⊙^{ce} at m.b. 1′ 6″). Black throughout, except some red on one side of the bottom.

92. *Jāḍi* (M/D-3½″, H-7″). Coarse, light red unpolished material. The pointed bottom is broken. Pl. VI, Fig. 33.

93. *Kuṇḍān* (M/D-5″, H-4″). Some original earth inside and a ring-stand below. One line runs around below the rim.

94. *Śithai* (M/D-1″, H-3¼″, ⊙^{ce} 1′ 5″). Small mouth. Red with traces of black outside. Pl. VI, Fig. 34.

95. *Kuṇḍān* (M/D-5″, H-4″). Some original earth inside and a ring-stand below. One line runs around below the rim.

96. *Pallāi* (M/D-4″, H-5″, ⊙^{ce} at m.b. 1′ 7″). Neck slightly broken. Three parallel lines run around, below the rim.

NOTE.—The majority of the remaining articles in pottery are black and red outside and black inside. Where it is otherwise the colour is noted.

97. *Kuṇḍu Bōgiṇi* (M/D-3″, H-5″). Almost black throughout.

98. *Śombu* (M/D-3″, H-3″, ⊙^{ce} 1′ 1″). There is a coating of earth inside. Greater part black, with a red bottom.

99. *Kuṇḍu Bōgiṇi* (M/D-2″, H-4″).

100. *Śiṇṇa Kalayam* (M/D-2½″, H-3″, ⊙^{ce} 1′). Black throughout.

101. *Mūḍi* (M/D-3$\frac{1}{2}$", H-2$\frac{3}{4}$"). Has a coating of lime both inside and outside.

102. *Śombu* (M/D-3", H-3").

103. Tumbler-shaped vessel (M/D-4", H-3$\frac{1}{2}$"). There is a slight coating of lime inside. Pl. VI, Fig. 35.

104. *Śombu* (M/D-2$\frac{1}{2}$", H-2$\frac{3}{4}$", $\odot^{ce}$ 11"). Unpolished, coloured red throughout.

105 and 106. *Mūsais* (M/D-2" each, H-4$\frac{1}{2}$" and 3$\frac{3}{4}$"). A ring-stand is below no. 106.

107. *Kalayam* (M/D-2$\frac{1}{2}$", H-2$\frac{1}{4}$", $\odot^{ce}$ 1').

108. *Kiṇṇam* (M/D-4", H-2$\frac{3}{4}$"). Two parallel lines run around below the rim. Dull red, with traces of black on the rim.

109. *Mūsai* (M/D-2", H-3"). Red throughout.

110. *Maravai* (M/D-4", H-3"). Concave below neck. Pl. VI, Fig. 36.

111. *Mūḍi* (M/D-4", H-2$\frac{1}{4}$"). Ring-stand below.

112. *Bōgiṇi* (M/D-2", H-2", $\odot^{ce}$ 10"). There is a ring-stand below.

113. *Kiṇṇam* (M/D-3$\frac{1}{2}$", H-2$\frac{1}{2}$"). Dull red throughout.

114. *Śombu* (M/D-2$\frac{1}{2}$", H-2", $\odot^{ce}$ 11"). Red throughout.

115. *Kalayam* (M/D-2", H-2$\frac{1}{2}$", $\odot^{ce}$ 10"). Has a pointed base.

116. *Kiṇṇam* (M/D-4", H-3").

117. *Mūsai* (M/D-2$\frac{1}{2}$", H-3$\frac{1}{2}$").

118 and 119. *Tālam* (M/D-3" each, H-1$\frac{1}{4}$" each). Pl. VI, Fig. 37.

120. *Kalayam* (M/D-2", H-2", $\odot^{ce}$ 11").

121. *Kiṇṇam* (M/D-3$\frac{1}{2}$", H-2$\frac{1}{2}$").

122. *Uruḷi* (M/D-3", H-2$\frac{1}{4}$"). Bottom pointed.

123 and 124. *Kalayams* (M/D-2$\frac{1}{2}$" and 2", H-3" and 2$\frac{1}{2}$", $\odot^{ce}$ 1' and 10"). Rim slightly broken in no. 123. Some earth in no. 124.

125. *Mūḍi* (M/D-3$\frac{1}{2}$", H-2$\frac{3}{4}$").

126. *Kalayam* (M/D-2", H-3$\frac{1}{2}$", $\odot^{ce}$ 1').

127. *Mūkku Kiṇṇam* (M/D-3", H-1$\frac{1}{4}$"). Colour red throughout. There is a small tube on one side so that the liquid contents may be poured through to feed children. Pl. VI, Fig. 38.

128. *Tālam* (M/D-2$\frac{1}{4}$", H-1$\frac{1}{4}$"). Black throughout.

129. Bowl (M/D-3", H-1$\frac{1}{2}$"). A beaded line around below the neck. Black throughout. Pl. VI, Fig. 39.

130. *Mūḍi* (M/D-4", H-1").

131. *Kalayam* (M/D-2$\frac{1}{2}$", H-3$\frac{1}{2}$", $\odot^{ce}$ 1').

132. *Uruḷi* (M/D-2$\frac{1}{2}$", H-3$\frac{1}{2}$"). Ring-stand below.

133 and 134. *Kuṇḍu Bōgiṇis* (M/D-3" and 3$\frac{1}{4}$", H-2" and 2$\frac{1}{4}$"). Ring-stand below no. 133.

135. *Pāli* (M/D-5", H-3", $\odot^{ce}$ at m.b. 6"). Bowl-shaped receptacle, separated by a narrow neck from a spreading base. Vessels such as this are used now-a-days on marriage occasions. Similar to no. 370.

136. *Tālam* (M/D-3″, H-1″). Black throughout.

137. *Mūḍi* (M/D-3″, H-2″).

138. *Uruḷi* (M/D-3″, H-2″).

139. *Paḷḷāi* (M/D-1½″, H-2½″, ⊙ce 9″). Red throughout.

140. *Kiṇṇam* (M/D-2¼″, H-1½″).

141. *Śaṭṭi* (M/D-1½″, H-1¾″). Some earth inside: the colour is red throughout.

142. *Uruḷi* (M/D-2½″, H-1½″).

143. *Bōgiṇi* (M/D-2¾″, H-2⅛″). Almost black throughout.

144. *Kiṇṇam* (M/D 3¼″, H-2¼″). Some earth inside: black throughout.

145. *Kuṇḍu Bōgiṇi* (M/D-2″, H-2″). Red throughout.

146. A set of miscellaneous small objects consisting of a *kammal* (ear ornament), *tali* * of elongated tubular form, several globular beads and other objects. There is also a toy *śombu*. Pl. VI, Fig. 40.

147. A set of miscellaneous small objects consisting of a toy bull, toy plate, a saucer lamp, a toy *śombu* and other articles.

NOTE.—Nos. 148 to 202 consist chiefly of fragmentary articles of pottery, but there are also a few stone articles. The geological names of the stones have been verified by M.R.Ry. H. Narayana Rao, Avargal, M.A., Lecturer in Geology, Presidency College, Madras. The pottery has been selected chiefly for the various forms of crude ornament applied.

148. Fragment of a large circular bowl-shaped vessel with a spout on the outside. The material is thin and made of fine clay; polished red on the exterior and black inside. Two incised parallel lines run around, below the rim (L-11″, B-7″, of spout M/D-1″, H-1¼″). Pl. VI, Fig. 41.

149. Potsherd (L-9″, B-6″). Rim of a large circular urn made of coarse red pottery. A double line of diagonal nail-marks runs around below the rim. Red material of medium thickness.

150. Potsherd (L-1½″, B-8″). Part of the body of an urn. Three parallel raised lines run round the outside. Colour red.

151. Black polished cylindrical stone pestle, of dark quartzite (L-6″, ⊙ce 8″). Through much use the body is concave except at the sides.

152. Potsherd (L-7″, B-6″). Fragment of an urn of coarse red material. On the inside is a projecting hook 7½″ in height, for suspending articles. Pl. VII, Fig. 1.

---

* A *tali* is worn by married women as part of a necklace. In modern times it is formed of metal, usually gold.

153. Cylindrical polished grey stone pestle (L-7″, ⊙ce 8″). Slightly concave. The ends are rough pointed and must have been enclosed in wood or metal.

154. Potsherd of red material. (L-2½″, B-¾″). Ornament of horse-shoe form similar to that on no. 162.

155. Potsherd (L-6″, B-5″). Part of the rim of a large circular urn. Below the roll-shaped rim are two raised drooping lines slightly spreading below. Coarse red thick material. Pl. VII, Fig. 2.

156. Potsherd (L-5½″, B-5″). Part of the rim of an urn with two lines of diagonal thumb-nail marks. Resembles no. 149, except that the nail-marks are in opposite directions.

157. Potsherd (L-8″, B-3¾″). Part of the rim of a very large urn Coarse red on the exterior and grey on the interior. Below the roll-shaped rim is a row of crude indentations made by finger tips. Pl. VII, Fig. 3.

158. Potsherd (L-6″, B-4¾″). Fragment of the rim of a large urn. The roll rim is away, but below its place is a raised double crescent. Material is coarse red, largely mixed with small stones. Pl. VII, Fig. 4.

159. Potsherd (L-6″, B-3¾″). This is a fragment of a *vānali* used for frying purposes. It has been bowl-shaped with a flat circular projection around the rim. Red thin material.

160. Potsherd (L-10″, B-3¾″). Part of the rim of an urn. The rim projects and has an incised line around it. Colour reddish grey. Thick coarse material.

161. Potsherd (L-7″, B-4½″). Similar to no. 152, but the hook is partly broken.

162. Potsherd (L-6″, B-6″). Part of the rim of an urn. Below the roll-shaped rim is a raised ornament like a two-pronged fork with rod below. Thick coarse red material, largely mixed with small stones; but a finer material has been applied to the surface. Pl. VII, Fig. 5.

163 to 165. Potsherd spouts. (M/D-1¾″ to 2″, H-1″ to 1½″, L-5″ to 3″, B-2½″ to 3¼″). Similar to no. 148. For no. 163, See Pl. VII, Fig. 6.

166. Potsherd with a hook about 3″ in height (L-6″, B-3¾″). Similar to no. 152.

167. A small broken grey quartzite pestle (L 3″, ⊙ce 7″).

168. Potter's clay implement (L 3″, ⊙ce 6″) or pestle used to tap unbaked pots while being shaped. This is of the form of a *śombu* but is solid. Pl. VII, Fig. 8.

169 and 170. Two quartzite grinding stones and two pestles (1″ ×5″, 5″ × 8″). Each of the stones is a rectangular slab with four legs of about 3″ in height. The pestles are cylindrical. The slab of no. 170 is much worn through long use. In no. 169, there is a slight cut on the top to rest the pestle. Pl, VII, Figs. 11 and 12.

171. Pipe (L-3″, ⊙ce 4½″). A passage runs through the body. It has been attached to some vessel.

172 and 173. Potsherds (L-5″, 3″, B-3¾″, 3″). Fragments of rims of urns ornamented with lines of diagonal nail-marks like no. 156.

174 to 177. Potsherds (L-3¾″ to 2¾″, B-1¼″ to ¾″). Parts of rims with projecting spouts like no. 163. No. 175 is double (M/D-1″ to 2″, H-1½″ to 2″). For no. 175, see Pl. VII, Fig. 13.

178. Potsherd (L-3″, B-3″). Part of a small round vessel. Ash coloured outside; but the material is apparently red.

179. A flat hollow knob which may have been attached to a lid. Grey. (H-2″, ⊙ce 5¾″).

180. Potsherd (L-6″, B-3″). Part of the rim of a large globular vessel. Below the rim is a series of convex and concave circular lines, with two rows of crudely formed wavy ornament below. Red. Pl. VII, Fig. 7.

181 to 188. Potsherds (L-9″ to 3″, B-6″ to 3″) with spouts (H-2″ to ½″, M/D-1¾″ to 1″) of various forms. All, with probably the exception of no. 185, have been attached to the outside rims of large urns of thin material. Like nos. 163 and 175. No. 185 is grey, the others are red.

189 and 190. Potsherds with leg (L-6″ to 2″, B-5½″ to 2″). Fragments of the bodies of large urns of coarse red material, each with a hook similar to no. 152.

191 to 197. Potsherds of the rims of large urns of coarse red pottery, showing various forms of lines of diagonal nail and finger impressions. (L-1′ 1″ to 6″, B-8″ to 3½″). Nos. 192 and 196 are interior ornaments, the others are on the outside. For no. 192, see Pl. VII, Fig. 18.

198. Potsherd (L-5″, B-5″, ⊙ce 1′ 2″). Apparently a fragment of a moulded roof terminal; the material is red-coloured, but covered with an ash-coloured deposit. It is not a sepulchral object but got from an adjoining village site.

199 to 202. Saucer lamps (M/D-6″ to 4½″, H-3″ to 2″). Each has a flat bottom. Colour red. For no. 200, see Pl. VII, Fig. 10.

203. Small *Pāṇai*. (M/D-4½″, H-6″, ⊙ce 1′ 11″). On the outside of the body a pair of incised parallel lines run around. Ring-stand below.

204 to **211.** *Tōṇḍis* (M/D-3¾″ to 4″, H-9″ to 11″, ⊙ce 2′ 6″ to 1′ 11″). Globular pots of red colour with a cylindrical neck. Traces of black in the neck of no. 207. Ring-stand below each.

212 to **218.** *Maikkiṇṇams* (M/D-1″ to 1¼″, H-¾″, to ¼″). All are of red material; but all have had a black polish (except no. 216) which is now mostly away except in the case of no. 214. For no. 212, see Pl. VII, Fig. 9.

219 and **220.** *Mūḍis* (M/D-2⅓″ to 2″, H-1½″ to ¾″). Both have been black and red, but the black is now almost away from no. 219.

221 to **224.** *Maikkiṇṇams* (M/D-2″ each, H-½″ to ⅜″). All are black on the surface, but the material is red.

225. *Mūḍi* (M/D-2″, H-⅜″). Black.

226. *Pallāi* (M/D-3″, H-4″, ⊙ce 1′ 3″). Globular bulging red body and black cylindrical neck; a circular stand below. Pl. VII, Fig 17.

227. *Kalyyam* (M/D-2¾″, H-3¾″, ⊙ce 1′ 2″). This has a pointed bottom. Black on red material; a circular stand below.

228 to **230.** *Maravais* (M/D-2¼″ to 2″, H-5″ to 4″). Black and red. Stands below.

231 to **234.** *Kalayams* (M/D-2″ to 1½″, H-4″ to 3½″, ⊙ce 11″ to 8″). Nos. 231 and 234 have long necks. Nos. 233 and 234 have *mūḍis*, on the top. No. 233, has, in addition to the *mūḍi*, an elongated neck. All are on stands. For no. 234, see Pl. VII, Fig. 15.

235. Bowl with a *mūḍi* (M/D-4″, H-3½″). This bowl has a pointed bottom with a ring stand below. Black colour. Pl. VII, Fig. 16.

236 to **241.** *Kalayams* (M/D-1″ each, H-3¼″ to 2¼″, ⊙ce 9″ to 7″). For no. 236, see Pl. VII, Fig. 14. Nos. 236 to 238 have long necks. No. 241 has a wide mouth, nearly as wide as the body. In no. 240 there is a hole in the middle of the body, probably intended as a *mūkku* (nose) for pouring out the contents. All these vessels have been of black or red material, but the former colour is mostly worn off.

242. *Śaṭṭi* (M/D-2″, H-2″). Has a wide mouth and a thick cylindrical rim. Red coloured.

243 and **244.** *Mūḍis* (M/D-1½″, 2″; H-1¾″, 2″). These are placed on ring-stands. Red with traces of black.

245. Cup with a pointed bottom (M/D-4″, H-4″). Red coloured with black inside and at the rim.

246. *Kiṇṇam* (M/D-3″, H-3″). Black, with a slight coating of chunam inside.

247. *Mūḍi* (M/D-1½″, H-1¾″). The knob is broken.

248 and **249.** *Kalayams* (M/D-1½″ each, H-5″, 5½″, ⊙ᶜᵉ 1′ 4″ and 1′ 5″). No. 248 has a pointed bottom. No. 249 is full of earth. Both have a globular body with small neck and are black coloured, with stands below. For no. 248, see. Pl. VII, Fig. 19.

250. *Maravai* (M/D-2½″, H-3″). Projecting rim; dull red.

251 and **252.** *Kuḍams* (M/D-3″, 4″; H-7″, 6½″; ⊙ᶜᵉ 1′ 11″, 1′ 7″). The former is dull red, and the latter a deep red, with a line running around the neck. Both have earth inside and stands below. For no. 252, see Pl. VII, Fig. 20.

253 to **255.** *Tōṇḍis* (M/D-3″ to 3½″, H-7″ to 8″, ⊙ᶜᵉ 1′ 11″ to 1′ 8″) with stands below each. Neck black in all. No. 254 is pale red and has earth inside.

256 to **262.** *Jāḍis* (M/D-3″ to 4″; H-7½″ to 10″, ⊙ᶜᵉ 1′ 2″ to 1′ 8″). No. 256 has a lid with a flat base and is black in colour throughout. It has a cylindrical *mūḍi* or cover, and in all respects is similar to some of the bronze jars, such as no. 5. It is a unique specimen. Nos. 257 to 259 are red-coloured with curving concave necks. In nos. 260 and 261 the neck is black and the body red; they rest on stands. For no. 256, see Pl. VII, Figs. 21 and 22 and for no. 262, see Pl. VII, Fig. 23.

263. *Kūja* (M/D-3½″, H-7½″, ⊙ᶜᵉ at m. b. 1′ 6″). This is intended for cooling water; it has a long neck and a bulbous body. There is a stand below. Pl. VII, Fig. 24.

264 to **271.** *Maikkiṇṇams* (M/D-2″ to 4″, H-½″ to ¾″). Nos. 267 and 271 are grey coloured and the rest black.

272 and **273.** *Pālis* (M/D-2″, 2½″; H-4″, 3¾″). The former has a broad base. They serve the purpose of stands. For no. 272, see Pl. VII, Fig. 25.

274 to **277.** *Kuḍam* (M/D-¾″ to 1″, H-4″ to 6″, ⊙ᶜᵉ 10″ to 1′ 2″). These have an elongated pointed bottom and a very narrow mouth. No. 277 is full of earth. They rest on stands: colour black. For no. 275, see Pl. VII, Fig. 28.

278 to **282.** *Pallāis* (M/D-2½″ to 4″, H-3″ to 5″, ⊙ᶜᵉ 11″ to 1′ 4″). These have a wide mouth and bulbous body. No. 279 is black, the rest are black and red. Nos. 279 and 280 are on stands.

283 to **289.** *Kalayams* (M/D-1½″ to 2″; H-3″ to 5″; ⊙ᶜᵉ 1′ to 7′). These are of various sizes, but generally small. They have a narrow neck and a bulbous body. Colours black and red. No. 284 is full of earth. Nos. 283 and 284 are on stands.

290. *Śorakkāi-lōṭṭā* (H-3¼″, ⊙ᶜᵉ at bottom 5½″, M/D-¾″). This has an elongated body with a small neck and resembles a *śorakkāi*.

Black colour, unpolished and of friable material. Pl. VII, Fig. 26.

291. *Agal* (M/D-2″, H-1¾″). An earthen lamp with a projection for the wick. Pl. VII, Fig. 29.

292 and **293.** *Mūkku Kinnams* (M/D-2½″, 2¾″; H-2″ each). A small tube on one side of the cup (L-½″ to ¾″) is for pouring out the contents or for feeding infants with milk. They may be compared with no. 127. The first is black and the second red. For no. 292 see Pl. VII, Fig. 30.

294. *Maravai* (M/D-2½″, H-2½″). Mouth nearly as wide as the body. Dull red.

295. *Tavalai* (M/D-3″, H-3½″, ⊙ce 9″). Wide concave neck and a pointed bottom. Red. Pl. VII, Fig. 27.

296. *Mūḍi* of small size without a knob; black coloured.

297. *Santhana Pēlā* (M/D-3″, H-5″). A long cup on a concave base, intended for keeping sandal, etc.; it has a black lid. Dull red. Pl. VII, Fig. 32.

298 and **299.** *Kuṇḍu Bōgiṇis* (M/D-2½″, 4″; H-4″, 6″). Colour black and red; each rests on a black ring-stand. No. 299 has a dotted diagonal ornament around the rim. Both have conical pointed lids.

300 and **301.** *Kiṇṇams* (M/D-3½″ each; H-4″, 4½″). Dull red with worn off traces of black; each is on a black ring-stand

302. Bowl with a pointed bottom (M/D-7″, H-6″). It is on a circular stand and is covered with a fine large lid. Lid and stand black; bowl black and red. Pl. VII, Fig. 33.

303. *Pāṇai* (M/D-5″, H-7″). Two incised lines run around below the neck. Colour black and red. It is on a black ring-stand.

304. *Jāḍi* (M/D-3″, H-5″, ⊙ceat bulging point 1′ 2″) with a pointed bottom. Red and black; covered with a black cup-shaped *mūḍi* and resting on a circular black stand. Pl. VII, Fig. 31.

305. *Maḍakku* (M/D-10″, H-4½″). A large bowl resting on a separate base. Red with black rim; base or stand black. Two incised lines run around the rim. It is filled with earth and pieces of mica. Pl. VII, Fig. 35.

306. *Mūḍi* (M/D-7″, H-4″). Rests on a black stand. Inside are fragments of bronze and mica. Black and red.

307. *Kuṇḍān* (M/D-7″, H-5″). Filled with bones. Colour black and red. On a black stand.

308 to **311.** *Kalayams* (M/D-3″ to 1½″, H-2″ to 4″). All except no. 310 rest on black stands. No. 311 has a cup-like *mūḍi*. Colour generally black and red, but the former is mostly worn off.

312. *Jāḍi* (M/D-5", H-7") with a lid and stand. The former is black and red and the two latter black. Pl. VII, Fig. 34.

313. *Kuṇḍu Bōgiṇi* (M/D-3", H-6"). Rests on a black stand. Colour black and red.

314. *Kiṇṇam* (M/D-5", H-$4\frac{1}{2}$") Black and red; rests on a black stand.

315 to 317. *Kalayams* (M/D-$2\frac{1}{2}$" to 2"; H-$1\frac{3}{4}$" to $2\frac{1}{4}$"). Colour black and red.

318 to 324. *Kuṇḍāns* (M/D-3", H-3"). Colour black and red.

325 and 326. *Kuḍuvais* (M/D-$1\frac{1}{2}$" each; H-9", 7"; $\odot^{ce}$ 1′9", 1′7"). The former is of a grey ash colour and the latter is black throughout. Both have a pointed bottom and narrow neck. They are on stands. For no. 325, Pl. VII, Fig. 36.

327. *Pāṇai* (M/D-$3\frac{1}{2}$"; H-10"; $\odot^{ce}$ 2′). Neck slightly broken. Black and red. Is on a stand.

328. *Kuḍam* (M/D-4"; H-8"; $\odot_{ce}$ 2′ 4"). Colour red; rests on a black stand.

329. *Pāṇai* (M/D-4"; H-6"; $\odot^{ce}$ 1′8"). It has a *mūḍi* (broken) with earth in the interspace. Red coloured throughout. Rests on a black stand.

330 to 332. *Maḍakkus* (M/D-6" to 1′; H-3" to $2\frac{1}{2}$"). Bowl-shaped vessels with similarly formed *mūḍis* which are embedded in the earth inside. Colour red. They rest on black stands.

333 and 334. *Jāḷis* (M/D-4" each; H-9", 10"; $\odot^{ce}$ 1′ 10", 2′ 2"). Have a rim at the mouth and parallel incised lines around the neck. Red colour. Both rest on stands.

335. *Kuṇḍān* (M/D-5", H-3"). Dull red; rests on a black stand.

336 and 337. *Maravais* on stands (M/D-3", 4"; H-7", 8"). In no. 336 a series of lines runs around below the rim; above the lines the colour is black, below it is dull red. No. 337 is red, but mottled with traces of black.

338 and 339. *Kalayams* on stands (M/D-5" each; H-6", 7"; $\odot^{ce}$ at middle belt 2′ 3"). No. 338 is of a dull red colour. No. 339 is black above and red below.

340. *Mūḍi* (M/D-1′, H-5"). This may be described as a cover, and it perhaps was one; but it is of wide bowl-shape and may possibly have been so used. It has earth inside. One portion of the top is broken. There is a ring-stand below.

341 and 342. *Tavalais* (M/D-$6\frac{1}{2}$", 6"; H-9", 7"; $\odot^{ce}$ 2′ 5", 1′ $11\frac{1}{2}$"). Both are dull red coloured, and rest on stands. For no. 341, see Pl. VII, Fig. 37.

343. *Kūja* with *mūḍi* (M/D-$4\frac{1}{2}$"; H-8"; $\odot^{ce}$ at m.b. 1′11"). It is slightly broken at the bottom and is full of earth. A stand below.

5

344 to **350**. *Kuṇḍu Bōginis* (M/D-2″ to 3″; H-4″ to 5″). Nos. 344, 346 and 348 have a lid and earth inside. All have stands below.

351. *Mūsai* (M/D-2″; H-4″). Upper half black and lower red. There is an elongated stand below.

352 to **355**. *Bōginis* (M/D-2½″ to 4″; H-2½″ to 3″). Nos. 354 and 355 are black, with lines below the rim. All are on stands. For nos. 353 and 355, see Pl. VII, Fig. 38 and Pl. VIII, Fig. 4, respectively.

356. *Mūḍi*, (M/D-3″, H-2½″). Conical shape. Pl. VIII, Fig. 5.

357 to **361**. *Kiṇṇams* (M/D-2″ to 3″; H-1½″ to 1¾″). Of various shapes, with and without moulded rims. No. 359 has a pointed bottom; no. 361 is black with a stout rim.

362 and **363**. *Agals* (M/D-2½″ to 3″; H-2″ each). Black throughout. For no. 362, see Pl. VII, Fig. 39.

364 and **365**. *Śiṇṇa Bōginis* (M/D-2″ each; H-2″ each). No. 364 is red, and no. 365 black and red.

366 and **367**. *Śoppus* (M/D 1″; H-1½″, 2″). Red.

368 and **369**. Lamp (M/D-3″ to 3¾″; H-1″ nearly). These earthen lamps have a spout at one side for the projecting wick. No. 368 is ornamented with incised lines on the rim. For no. 369, see Pl. VIII, Fig. 6.

370. *Pāli* (M/D-5½″, H-3½″, ⊙ce at m.b. 7″). This resembles a ring-stand, but has no hole through the centre as they have. It is a flat vase. Pl. VIII, Fig. 3.

371 to **377**. *Tōṇḍis*, (M/D-3½″ to 4″, H-9″ to 11″, ⊙ce at m.b. 2′ 2″, 2′7″). These are generally of one form, but vary in minor particulars. They are all of varying shades of dull red. All are on stands. For no. 373, see Pl. VIII, Fig. 1.

378. *Śaṭṭi* (M/D-4½″, H-6″, ⊙ce at m.b. 1′ 11″). Moulded lines around the neck. It is full of earth and has a stand below. Pl. VIII, Fig. 9.

379. *Kalayam* (M/D-4″, H-7″, ⊙ce at m.b. 2′ 1″). Rim slightly broken. Dull blackish red throughout. There is a stand below.

380 to **386**. *Kuṇḍu Bōginis* (M/D 3″ to 2½″, H-4″ to 5″). Nos. 380, 383, 385 and 386 have lids. All have stands below.

387 to **389**. Cups with round or slightly pointed bottoms (M/D-4″ to 3″, H-3½″ to 3″). Black and red, with stands below.

390 to **397**. *Mūḍis* (M/D-3″ to 2½″, H-2″ to 1½″).

398. *Kiṇṇam* (M/D-2½″, H-1″). Black coloured, with a thick rim.

399 and **400**. *Mūsais* (M/D-2″ and H-7″ each). For no. 399, see Pl. VIII, Fig. 2.

401 to **409.** *Tōṇḍis* (M/D-3½" to 4"; H-7" to 1'; ⊙ᶜᵉ at m.b. 1' 8" to 2' 7"). No. 403 has a coating of lime or *chunam*. Nos. 404, 406 and 409 are black at the top. All have ring-stands below.

410. *Jāḍi* (M/D-5"; H-7"; ⊙ᶜᵉ at m.b. 1' 7"). Rounded conical base; black and red. There is a stand below. Pl. VIII, Fig. 10.

411 and **412.** *Mūḍis* (M/D-7"; H-4" each) with another imbedded in earth contained in no. 411. No. 412 contains bones and a small cup-like vessel.

413 and **414.** *Kuṇḍu Bōgiṇis* (M/D-2½" to 3": H-4" each). Both have stands below, and no. 413 has a lid.

415. *Maravai* with a lid and stand. (M/D-3" : H-4").

416. Cup with lid and stand. (M/D-4" : H-2½").

417 to **421.** *Śoppus* (M/D-1" to 1½": H-2¾" to 2"). No. 418 is full of earth.

422 to **426.** *Kiṇṇams* (M/D-2½" to 3" : H-2" each).

427 to **429.** *Mūsais* (M/D-2" each : H-7" to 8"). All have stands below.

430. *Śoppu* on a high ring-stand. (M/D-2" : H-2½"). It contains earth.

431 to **438.** *Kuṇḍu Bōgiṇis* (M/D-4" to 5" : H-5" to 6"). No. 433 is full of earth and is ornamented by dots on the neck. Nos. 431, 433, 434, 437 and 438 have lids ornamented with dotted lines, either incised or marked with colour. All have stands below.

439. Bowl with conical bottom (M/D-10" : H-6"). Inside are bones, an elongated ring-stand and an *agal*. It has a stand below.

440. Broken bowl with three long ring-stands embedded in the earth inside (M/D-7" : H-4"). It has a ring-stand below. Pl. VIII, Fig. 13.

441 to **446.** Parts of lids. These illustrate various forms of lid terminals. (H-3" to 4"). For nos. 443 to 446, see Pl. VIII, Figs. 8, 12, 14 and 18.

447. *Śembu* (M/D-2" : H-4"). With a stand below.

448. *Mūḍi* (M/D-5" : H-3"). The inside is black. It rests on a stand.

449 and **450.** *Kuṇḍāns* (M/D-3" each : H-3" each). Both have ring-stands below (3"). There is earth inside no. 450.

451. *Vānali* (M/D-3" : H-2"). The inside is black. It has a lid above and a stand below.

452 to **454.** *Kuṇḍu Bōgiṇis* (M/D-2" to 2½": H-4" to 5"). All have stands below.

455 to **462.** *Maikkiṇṇams* (M/D-1" to 2": H-1" nearly each). Nos. 460 to 462 are red in colour and the rest black.

463. *Kūja Mūḍi* (M/D-1½": B-3": H-½").

464. *Kiṇṇam* with rim (M/D-2½": H-1"). Black coloured.

465. *Tavalai* (M/D-3″: H-2½″: ⊙ce at m.b. 10½″). Neck broken; there is a ring-stand below.

466 to **473.** *Tōṇḍis* (M/D-3″ to 5″: H-8″ to 1′: ⊙ce at m.b. 1′ 10″ to 2′ 10″). Nos. 469 and 470 are full of earth; all are dull red coloured. All have stands below. For no. 466, see Pl. VIII, Fig. 15.

474 and **475.** *Bōgiṇis* (M/D-1½″ each: H-1½″ each). No. 475 is black in colour.

476. *Marakkāl* (M/D-6″: H-5″). With a cylindrical neck over a bulbous conical body. This class of vessel is used for measuring grain. There is a stand below. Pl. VIII, Fig. 17. Similar to no. 553.

477. *Mūsai* (M/D-2″: H-5″). This has an elongated ring-stand.

478 to **481.** Cups with pointed base (M/D-3″ to 4″: H-3″ to 5″). No. 480 has a coating of *chunam*. All have stands below; and the one for no. 481 is elongated.

482 and **483.** *Bōgiṇis* (M/D-3″ and 4″: H-2¾″ and 3″). With stands below.

484 to **486.** *Kuṇḍu Bōgiṇis* (M/D-2″ to 2½″: H-2″ to 2½″).

487. *Śiṇṇa Śaṭṭi* (M/D-1″: H-2″). Black coloured.

488. *Kūja Mūḍi* (M/D-1″: H-2″).

489 and **490.** *Kalayams* (M/D-2″, 2½″: H-2½″, 3½″: ⊙ce 9″, 11½″). Neck broken in both. The former is red and the latter partly red and black. No. 489 has a stand below.

491. *Pāṇai* (M/D-5″: H-9″: ⊙ce at m.b. 2′ 2″). With a stand below.

492. *Śaṭṭi* (M/D-5″: H- 9″: ⊙ce 2′ 5″). With a stand below.

493 to **495.** *Tōṇḍis* (M/D-3″ to 5″: H-8″ to 1′). All have stands below.

496. *Pāṇai* (M/D-4″, H 9″, ⊙ce at m.b. 2′ 2″). With a stand.

497. *Kuḍam* (M/D-6″, H-10″, ⊙ce at m.b. 2′ 3″). Red coloured and highly polished; with a stand.

498. *Tavalai* (M/D-5″; H-7″, ⊙ce 2′ 2″). Neck broken and top portion black. There is a stand below.

499. Lid (H-2″, ⊙ce 7½″). On a ring-stand below.

500. Small bowl with a pointed base (M/D-6″, H-3″). Black coloured with a ring-stand below.

501. *Tāḷam* (M/D-10″; H-2½″). There are bones inside. Pl. VIII, Fig. 11.

502. Bowl with a cylindrical neck and a pointed base (M/D-4½″, H-4½″). Black throughout. Pl. VIII, Fig. 19.

503. *Kuṇḍu Bōgiṇi* (M/D-2″, H-4″). On a stand.

504. *Maravai* (M/D-3½″, H-6″). On a stand. The rim is slightly broken; some incised-lines run around below the neck.

505 to **508.** *Mūsais* (M/D-2″ to 2½″, H-5½″ to 7″). No. 507 is full of earth and no. 505 has a pointed bottom. All have stands below.

509. *Pallāi* (M/D-4½″, H-7″, ⊙ce 1′ 10″). On a stand.

510. *Śaṭṭi* (M/D-4½″, H-6″, ⊙ 1′ 8″). On a stand. Red.

511 to **513.** *Jādis* (M/D-3″ to 2½″, H-8″ each, ⊙ce 1′ 8″ to 1′ 11″). No. 511 is black at the neck, nos. 512 and 513 are red. Not a surface colour but due to burning. All have stands below.

514. *Kalayam* (M/D-4″, H-7½″, ⊙ce 2′ 2″). This has a dull red colour. There is a stand below.

515. Large bowl with slightly pointed base (M/D-1′, H-7″), resting on a small stand. Black coloured with mottled red below. There are bones inside. Pl. VIII, Fig. 16.

516 to **520.** *Mūsais* (M/D-2″ to 2½″, H-3″ to 5″). Nos. 516 to 518 are on elongated stands. For no. 520, see Pl. VIII, Fig. 20.

521 and **522.** *Bōgiṇis* (M/D-3″ to 5″, H-2½″ to 4″). Both have stands below.

523 to **527.** *Uruḷis* (M/D-3″ to 4″, H-2½″ each). Nos. 523 and 524 have a tapering pointed base. No. 525 has a coating of *chunam* ; nos. 526 and 527 are of a dull red colour. All except no. 523 are on stands.

528. *Jāḍi* (M/D-3″, H-5″, ⊙ce 1′ 2″). There is a stand below.

529. *Uruḷi* with pointed bottom (M/D-4½″, H-3″). It has a lid above and a stand below. Pl. VIII, Fig. 21.

530 and **531.** *Kiṇṇams* (M/D-3½″ each, H-3″ nearly each). The former has a rim of bead section, and the latter a cylindrical neck.

532 to **536.** *Kuṇḍu Kiṇṇams* (M/D-2″ to 2½″, H-1½″ each). There is a slight coating of *chunam* on nos. 532 and 533.

537 to **543.** *Maikkiṇṇams* (M/D-1½″ to 2″, H-½″ each). Black coloured.

544. *Kūja Mūḍi* (B-3″). Slightly broken.

545. *Śoppu* (M/D-2½″, H-2½″). Red ; rim slightly chipped.

546 to **549.** *Toṇḍis* on stands (M/D-4″ to 5½″, H-7″ to 9″. ⊙ce 1′ 8″ to 2½′). Rim slightly broken in all. Dark red colour. No. 549 has a short neck (3″).

550. *Maravai* (M/D-4″, H-8″, ⊙ce 1′ 9″). Dark red colour ; on a stand.

551 and **552.** *Kalayams* (M/D-2″ to 3½″, H-3″ to 6″, ⊙ce at m.b. 9½″ to 1′ 7″). Black ; the neck in no. 551 is slightly broken. Both have stands below.

553. *Marakkāl* with a pointed bottom (M/D-7″, H-7″). On a stand. Broken at the top ; with earth inside, containing two other small pieces of pottery in their original positions. Pl. VIII, Fig. 23.

554 and **555.** *Mūsais* (M/D-2″, 2½″: H-4½″, 5½″). Both of a grey red colour.

556 and **557.** Flat cups (M/D-2″, 3″ : H-1½″, 2″). The former is red.

558 and **559.** *Bōgiṇis* (M/D-3″ each : H-nearly 1½″ each).

560 to 562. Small wide cups with a slightly pointed bottom (M/D-3½" to 4½": H-2½" to 3").

563. *Mūḍi* (M/D-4", H-2"). Black coloured.

564. *Mūḍi* (H-3", M/D-5"). There are small objects inside; red coloured, with a coating of ash.

565. Bowl with slightly pointed bottom (M/D-6", H-4"). Neck concave.

566. Bottom of a large stand (H-7"). Thick red, unpolished pottery (⊙ce at bottom 1' 10½"). Pl. VIII, Fig. 28.

567. Large cup with a wide mouth and a flat bottom (M/D-4½", H-4"). Over it is a lid with an unusual cup terminal and a stand below. Pl. VIII Fig. 25.

568. *Mūḍi* (M/D-6", H-3"). On a ring-stand; black inside.

569. *Pāli* (M/D-7", H-5", ⊙ce at m.b. 6½"). Vase-shaped bowl on a stand, all in one piece. Pl. VIII, Fig. 22.

570. *Mūḍi* (M/D-1', H-4"). With a ring-like knob inside for lifting it. Red unpolished pottery. The only specimen of its class found. It is placed on a stand. Pl. VIII, Fig. 26.

571. Cup with pieces of mica inside (M/D-7", H-4"). Slightly broken at one part. Dull black colour. There is a stand below.

572. Bowl with pieces of hæmatite inside (M/D-10", H-4"). Rests on a ring-stand.

573. Bowl with pieces of mica inside (M/D-8", H-5"). On a ring-stand. Both black.

574. Bowl with earth inside, containing another small piece of pottery (M/D-7", H-4"). On a stand.

575 to 578. *Tōṇḍis* (M/D-3" to 4", H-8' to 1', ⊙ce 1' 8½" to 2' 11"). All are dark red and have stands below. For no. 578, see Pl. VIII, Fig. 27.

579. *Pallāi* (M/D-4", H-6", ⊙ce 1' 11½"). Bell neck; has a ring around it, and is therefore unusual. There is a ring-stand below. Pl. VIII, Fig. 24.

580 to 586. *Kuṇḍu Bōgiṇis* (M/D-3" to 4", H-4" to 6"). On ring-stands. Nos. 580, 582 and 584 to 586 have lids. For no. 586, see Pl. VIII, Fig. 29.

587 and 588. *Siṇṇa Kuṇḍu Bōgiṇis* (M/D-2½", 3": H-4" each). Both have lids and stands.

589. *Mūsai* (M/D-2", H-6½").

590. *Kalayam* (M/D-3¾", H-4", ⊙ce 1' 4"). The lid has an unusual terminal and is broken on one side. There is a stand below.

591. *Jāḍi* (M/D-3½", H-7"). On a ring-stand.

592 and 593. *Kalayams* (M/D-2½", 3"; H-6", 7"; ⊙ce 1' 6½", 1' 9½"). Both have a fine polished black colour and are on stands.

594 to **597**. Lids (H-4″ to 5″, $\odot_{ce}$ at bottom 9″ to 1′ 2″). All have terminals of unusual form. Pl. VIII, Fig. 30. The terminal of no. 594 is pointed oval; no. 595 is cup-shaped; nos. 596 and 597 are pointed conical. All are black except no. 596 which has a coating of earth.

598. Fragment of wood found in an urn (L-1′ 5″, B-9″).

599. Two large red *pāṇais* over a pair of black ring-stands (H-11″, $\odot^{ce}$ 2′ 5″).

600. Red *Tōṇḍi* over a pair of black ring-stands; neck broken (H-1′, $\odot^{ce}$ 2′ 7″).

601. Dull red *Tōṇḍi* over a pair of black ring-stands (H-10″, $\odot^{ce}$ 2′ 8″).

602. Red *Pāṇai* and *Tōṇḍi* over a pair of black ring-stands (H-1′ 11″, $\odot^{ce}$ 2′ 8″).

603. *Jāḍi* with neck broken. There are a pair of ring-stands below. Inside black, with broad mouth. (M/D-6″: $\odot^{ce}$ at m.b. 3′: H-1′). Pl. VIII, Fig. 7.

604. *Tōṇḍi* with a pair of ring-stands below. (M/D-4″: $\odot^{ce}$ 2′ 8″: H-1′).

605. *Pāṇai* with earth inside. This rests on a pair of ring-stands. (M/D-4″: H 11″: $\odot^{ce}$ at m.b. 2′ 7″).

606. *Tōṇḍi* with a pair of ring-stands below. Neck slightly broken (M/D-$4\frac{1}{2}$″, H-11″, $\odot^{ce}$ 2′ 8″).

607. *Tōṇḍi* with a pair of ring-stands below. This has a coating of *chunam*. From Korkai (M/D-$5\frac{1}{2}$″, H-9″, $\odot^{ce}$ 2′ 8″).

608. *Jāḍi* with a pair of ring-stands below. Neck slightly broken. (M/D-4″, H-1′ 2″, $\odot^{ce}$ 2′ 10″).

609. *Jāḍi* of a dark red colour with ring-stands below. (M/D-5″, H-1′ 1″, $\odot^{ce}$ 3′ 3″).

610. *Jāḍi* of a light red colour on ring-stands (M/D-4″, H-1′ 1″, $\odot^{ce}$ 2′ 9″).

611 to **616**. Pyriform-shaped urns varying in height from 2′ 2″ to 3′, and $\odot^{ce}$ from 5′ 3″ to 7′ 4″. The urns taper to a narrow flat bottom. All have a thick round beaded rim at the mouth. Nos. 611, 612 and 613 are examples of the ordinary form of urn. No. 614 is a different form with a bell mouth, not so usual as the preceding; it also has a thumb-mark ornament around the rim and three raised streamers below the rim on one side. All these urns are of coarse thick red pottery. No. 615 (adjoining 614) follows the ordinary form of no. 611, but is of thin finer material and shows traces of black colour polish around the rim. No. 616 is an extra large urn of the usual form, but it has a circular raised band around the upper part, indented with finger-point impressions. At one side this band terminates in two reverse curves. On the interior six inches below the rim, at one side of the urn are two curved hooks of one and a half inches in length, placed nine inches apart. These are intended for the suspension of some of the small articles. For nos. 611, 615 and 616, see Pl. IX, Figs. 1, 2 and 3.

HUMAN BONES.

In two cases will be found a selection of skulls and other human bones from Ādichanallūr.

PERUMBĀIR PREHISTORIC ANTIQUITIES.

INTRODUCTION.*

Description of the excavations.†—There are a large number of rude stone monuments in the Chingleput district, several of which have been excavated. Mr. Sewell states (Lists of Antiq. Vol. I, p. 172) that these are probably relics of the Kurumbars, whose sovereigns belonged to the Pallava family and who once inhabited this part of the country prior to the eleventh century, when they were conquered by the Chōḷas. The popular name of *Kurumbar Mēḍū, i.e.*, Kurumbar mounds, given to such monuments, tends to confirm this statement.

I visited Perumbāir, strictly Perumbayūr, in the Madurāntakam taluk in 1904-05, and observing extensive groups of rude stone circles situated around the adjoining hills, decided on excavating some of them. The work was continued at intervals till 1907-08, and resulted in a very fair collection of prehistoric remains which differ in many respects from those pertaining to Tinnevelly.

The sites occur in the waste or rocky places (Pl. XIV, Fig. 1) which surround the range of hills above referred to, and the whole range is classed as a Government Reserve forest. Around the base of the hills the remains are placed a short distance from the bottom slopes, and usually consist of stone circles varying from eight to fifty feet in diameter, formed of rough stone boulders. In others, the stones have been removed and the site of deposit is only marked by a low mound, which must at one time have been much higher, but has been reduced in height by the action of the weather. In the centre of each stone circle is deposited either a pyriform urn or an elongated pottery cist.

The reservation of the site has been the means of protecting the majority of the remains from the unrestricted depredations of treasure seekers, and the result is that many of the circles contain deposits in a varying state of preservation. Such mounds as are outside the reserve, usually show traces of having been dug into. The mounds are generally covered with a dense growth of prickly-pear which has

* *Vide* Reports of the Archæological Survey, Southern Circle, 1905-06 and 1907-08, and the Archæological Survey of India, 1908-09, pp. 92-99.

† Though the name of the village has been adopted as the title of the site, it does not imply that these remains were found only in its vicinity. Excavation was first begun there and the seven other villages, where it was conducted, encircle the hills.

afforded another means of protection. The surface soil is a coarse gravel, with a substratum of clay of a red ferruginous kind. This is an unsuitable soil for the preservation of ceramic relics, as its expansion and contraction, according to the moisture to which it is subjected, result in the fracture of the pottery ; and the greatest difficulty has been experienced in restoring to shape the broken cists and urns that were brought to the Museum.

The deposits are found at a depth of two to seven feet below the surface and are contained in pyriform urns, or in oblong pottery cists or sarcophagi rounded at the ends and standing on three rows of short legs. The cists vary in length from two to seven feet and resemble those found at the Pallāvaram prehistoric site in the Saidāpet taluk, Chingleput district, excepting that those from the latter place invariably have two rows of legs, while those at Perumbāir, whether large or small, almost always have three.

The main deposits are found in the cists themselves, but as at the other sites, subsidiary deposits of pottery and iron implements are found outside and around them. Some of the smaller articles appear close to the surface and at intervals down to the main deposit, which may be as much as seven feet from the surface, but the depth is generally less.

The finds consisted of stone and iron implements and weapons, pottery, bones, and shell ornaments. In one cist was a human skeleton in a cross-legged sitting posture, with the hands resting on the knees as if in meditation. This, however, seems to be a comparatively modern interment and not of the prehistoric period. The condition of the bones shows this clearly, and the presence of a small black stone image of Ganēśa further confirms it. It has been the custom in certain exceptional cases to effect such recent burials in prehistoric sites.

POTTERY.

NOTE.—When compared with the Tinnevelly pottery, the difference in material and also to a certain extent in form is strikingly apparent. The material as a rule coarser, and specimens with the fine black and red glaze so common on the Tinnevelly objects are comparatively rare. Many are covered with a deposit of ash or lime. These Perumbāir exhibits mostly consist of pottery, but there are a few examples of stone and iron objects also.

1. *Jāḍi* Red coloured, with incised lines running around the body (H-6″, B-4″, M/D-4″). Pl. X, Fig. 1.
2. *Śaṭṭi* (H-5½″, B-9″, M/D-5″).
3. *Pallāi* (H-5½″, B-8″, M/D-4″). Red with a coating of ash. Pl. X, Fig. 2.

4 and 5. *Kuṇḍu Bōgiṇis* (H-4″, 3″; B-4½″, 4″). Ash coloured with traces of black appearing through. For no. 4, Pl. X, Fig. 3.

6 and 7. *Kuḍuvais* (H-5″, B-6″, M/D-3″, and H-3″, B-4½″, M/D-2″). No. 6 is dull red, and no. 7 has its mouth black, but is otherwise of an ash colour. For no. 7, see Pl. X, Fig. 4.

8 and 9. *Kalayams* (H-3″, B-5″, M/D-2″, and H-2½″, B-3″, M/D-1″). No. 8 is full of earth, and no. 9 has its mouth broken. Both are dull red.

10. Bowl with a pointed bottom (H-4″, M/D-5¾″). Inside black, upper part of outside black and lower part red. Pl. X, Fig. 6.

11. *Mondai* (H-6″, B-3½″, M/D-3″). Is full of earth. Coarse red material. There is a black projection below the neck for fixing a *mūḍi* or cover. Pl. X, Fig. 7.

12 and 13. *Bōgiṇis* (H-2″, M/D-4″, and H-3″, M/D-4¼″). Both are of ash colour. In no. 12 the neck is slightly black, and no. 13 is full of earth.

14. *Śaṭṭi* (H-4″, B-7″, M/D-4¾″). Dull red.

15. *Uruli* (H-2″, M/D-4″). Has a wide bell mouth. Ash colour. Pl. X, Fig. 5.

16. *Kalayam* (H-3½″, B-4″, M/D-1½″). Resembles nos. 8 and 9. Ash colour.

17. *Kuḍuvai,* (H-3½″, B-4½″, M/D-3″). Similar to nos. 6 and 7. Red with a coating of ash. There is a ring-stand below.

18. *Pāṇai* with *mūḍi* (H-4″, B-5″, M/D-3″). Ash colour. Pl. X, Fig. 8.

19. Tumbler (H-5″, M/D-4″). Ash colour. There is also a *mūḍi* on it. Pl. X, Fig. 9.

20 and 21. *Mondais* (M/D-3″, H-5″, B-3½″). These were found lying outside the end of cist no. 169. They resemble no. 11 but are of better make. Dull red colour. For no. 21. Pl. X. Fig. 10.

22 to 24. Tumblers (M/D-4½″ to 4″, H-5″ to 4″, B-4¾″ to 4″). Similar to no. 19. Ash colour. For no. 23, see Pl. X, Fig. 11.

25. *Pāṇai* (M/D-4½″, H-4″, B-5″). Ash colour.

26. *Kiṇṇam* (H-3″, B-4″). Is of thin material and has been black coloured, but is coated with ash. Pl. X, Fig. 12.

27. *Kuḍuvai* (M/D-3″, H-4″, B-4½″). Similar to nos. 6 and 7. Dull red.

28. *Kalayam* (M/D-2″, H-3″, B-4½″). Similar to nos. 9 and 16; there is earth inside. Neck broken. Dull red.

29. *Kuṇḍu Bōgiṇi* (H-4½″, B-4″). There are earth and bones inside. Traces of black polish appear through a thick ashy deposit.

30. *Kuḍuvai* (M/D-3″, H-4″, B-5″). A variety of no. 27. Dull red covered with ash. Pl. X, Fig. 13.

31. Tumbler (H-4″, B-4″). A part of the top broken. Thin red material with a black polish, almost wholly covered with ash.

32. *Kiṇṇam*, (M/D-4″, H-3″). Dull red.

33. *Kalayam* (M/D-2″, H-4″, B-5″). There is earth inside. Neck partly broken. Grey colour.

34. *Śithai* (M/D-1″, H-4″, B-8″). Neck broken, with incised lines radiating around it. Has a hole and marks on one side for a spout or handle. There is an incised ornamented base at the bottom. Grey ash colour. Pl. X, Fig. 14.

35 to **37.** *Tōṇḍis* (M/D-3″ to 2½″, H-6½″ to 4″, B-8″ to 4″). Nos. 35 and 37 have earth inside. Dull red colour.

38. *Śoppu* (M/D-3½″, H-3″). Upper half black and bottom red. There is earth inside.

39. *Kiṇṇam* with overlapping mouth. (M/D-4″, H-2½″). There is earth inside. Thin black coloured material covered with a grey deposit. Pl. X, Fig. 15.

40. *Agal* (M/D-4½″, H-1″). Black, covered with ash. Pl. X, Fig. 16.

41 and **42.** *Bōgiṇis* (M/D-4½″, 4″, H-3½″, 3″). Thin material with ashy deposit and traces of ash appearing through it.

43. Ring-stand (M/D-8″, H-5″). Of thick material covered with a deposit of lime. Pl. X, Fig. 17.

44. Bowl with a flat bottom (M/D-6″, H-3″). Dull grey colour. Pl. X, Fig. 18.

45. *Pāṇai* (M/D-4″, H-3″). There is earth inside. Ash colour with traces of black appearing at the rim. Pl. X, Fig. 19.

NOTE—Most of the exhibits numbered 46 to 167 are pottery, but there are a few in iron, stone and shell. The geological names of the stones have been verified by M.R.Ry. H. Narayana Rao Avargal, M.A., Lecturer in Geology, Presidency College.

46 to **52.** *Kuḍams* (M/D-11½″ to 8″, H-7½″ to 5½″). Wide flat body with cylindrical neck. All are dull red and coated with a grey deposit. No. 46 is dull red only. For nos. 46 and 50, see Pl. X, Figs. 20 and 21.

53 and **54.** *Kuḍuvais* (M/D-4″ to 3″, H-8″ to 6″). Moulded cylindrical neck. Grey colour. For no. 53, see Pl. X, Fig. 22.

55 to **57.** *Pallāis* (M/D 8½″ to 8″, H-8″ to 6″). They have cylindrical necks similar to nos. 46 to 52, but the body is more globular in form. Grey colour. For no. 57, see Pl. X, Fig. 23.

58 and **59.** *Pāṇais* (M/D-10″ and 9″, H-7″ and 5½″). These are wide-mouthed vessels. Grey colour.

60. *Śaṭṭi* (M/D-6″, H-5½″). Grey. Plate XI, Fig. 1.

61. *Kuḍuvai* (M/D-9″, H-6″). Grey colour.

2 and 63. *Tōṇḍis*, ($\odot^{ce}$ of body 9" and 8", H-7" and 6"). Both have lids. Colour red, covered with grey.

64. *Kuḍam* (M/D-5", H-4"). Dull red.

65. *Kalayam* (M/D-5", H-4").

66. Jar with three legs. (M/D-6", H-5½"). One side broken; coated with lime and filled with earth. Pl. XI, Fig. 2.

67 and 68. *Mūḍis* (M/D-7" and 6½"). Saucer-shaped. The first is dull red, the second is coated with lime.

69 to 71. *Agals* (M/D-4" and 3").

72. *Bōgiṇi* (M/D-4", H-5", $\odot^{ce}$ at m.b. 1'-5"). Coated with lime.

73. *Kalayam* (H-2", B-1½"). Dull black colour; is filled with earth.

74. *Kammal* (H-1", B-2"). An earthen ear ornament. Pl. XI, Fig. 3.

75. Potter's implement of sandstone (D-3¼"). Circular mass, convex on one side and flat on the other. Pl. XI, Fig. 4.

76 to 93. Toys. (small cup-shaped objects). Grey colour. For no. 85, see Pl. XI, Fig. 5.

94 to 122. Potsherds (3" to 1"). These are fragments of jars and large vessels, showing various forms of crude ornament, usually thumb and nail impressions, but some also in relief. These ornaments generally appear on the neck of the vessel. The colour is red, with in most cases a coating of lime. For nos. 94, 96, 97, 104, 105, 108, see Pl. XI, Figs. 6 to 11.

123 and 124. Conch shells (D-3½", L-7"). Ornamented with incised straight lines, with circles at the intersections. For no. 124, see Pl. XI, Fig. 12.

125 to 127. Iron hatchets. (L-1" to 6": B-4" to 3".) Broad flat metal, rounded at the butt end and broad at the cutting end. Somewhat similar to those from Tinnevelly. For no. 127, see Pl. XI, Fig. 13.

128. Scythe (L-11¾", B-of blade 1½"). Pl. XI, Fig. 14.

129 and 130. Iron arrow-heads with butt. (L-3½" to 4", Blade ½" to ⅓").

131. A block of manganese ore. Pl. XI, Fig. 15.

132. Iron hatchets (L-6½", B-2½").

133 and 134. Iron chisels (L-11" to 8": B-2" to 1¾"). The former is of thick and the latter of broad thin metal, resembling an elongated hatchet. For no. 134, see Pl. XI, Fig. 17.

135 and 136. Circular conch shell ornaments, with linear and circular ornamentation engraved and coloured. Each has a hole in the middle. These were probably used as head ornaments by women. (D-3", 2½"). Pl. XI, Figs. 19 and 24.

137. Conch shell ornament (L-3"). Made from the core of a shell. Linear engraved ornament; dark coloured. Pl. XI, Fig. 30.

138. Neolithic quartzite celt of polished grey stone (4" × 1¾"). Pl. XI, Fig. 20.

139. Roughly sculptured *Ganēśa* image of hardened clay (H-3½", B-2⅛"). It was found in a burial mound which is subsequent to the pre-historic period. Pl. XI, Fig. 16.

140. Ferruginous quartzite grinding slab with four legs (H-7", B-8", L-1′ 6"). Two of the legs at one end are broken. Pl. XI, Fig. 18.

141. Wide bowl of greyish red pottery (D-8", H-2½"). Some bone fragments are placed in it.

142 and **143.** *Kalayams* (D-3¼" and 2¼", H-3¼" and 2"). The first is black and the other red. For no. 142, see Pl. XI, Fig. 21.

144. Wide cup with rim (M/D-5", H-4"). Red colour.

145 to **147.** Knobs for lids (H-1½", 3" and 1"). Nos. 145 and 147 are black and no. 146 ash coloured. For no. 146, see Pl. XI, Fig. 22.

148. Grey granite roller (D-3½", L-8½"). Knob entire at one end, broken at the other. Pl. XI, Fig. 25.

149. Trap rock pounder (D-3", H-4½"). Cylindrical with knob on top. Pl. XI, Fig. 23.

150. Quartzite grinder (L-6", B-3"). Rectangular in section, slightly tapering to one end. One side smooth, others rough. Pl. XI, Fig. 26.

151. Dark green hornblende pounder (L-7", B-3"). Irregular oval section, rounded at one end, slightly tapering to the other. Finger and thumb gripping places on two sides.

152. Limestone grinder (L-4", B-3"). Oval section, projection at one end; other end broken.

153. Serpentine pounder (L-4½", B-2"). Square section, slightly tapering to one end; four sides smooth and polished; two ends rough. Pl. XI, Fig. 27.

154. Dark green quartzite roller (L-5", B-2"). Cylindrical. Pl. XI, Fig. 29.

155. Quartzite pounder (L-6", B-4"). Ovoid. Pl. XI, Fig. 28.

156. Earthy slate slab (L-7½", B-4½"). Rough irregular; small concavity for grinding powder on one side.

157. Quartzite hone (L-9", B-3½"). Rectangular section, slightly tapering. Smooth and polished on two sides.

158. Quartzite haematite hone (L-4½", B-2½"). Roughly rectangular; rubbed smooth on two sides.

159. Stone slab (L-4", B-3½"). Has a concavity on one side. Similar to but smaller than no. 156.

160. Fragment of a trap rock mortar (B-6"). Has been of circular form; polished on top.

161. Jar with three legs (H-1′ 9", D-11", Legs-8"). Top portion broken. Red pottery with lime coating. Pl XII, Fig. 1.

162. *Tōṇḍi* (M/D-4″, D-10½″, H-11″). Red pottery covered with a thick deposit of lime. It rests on no. 163.

163. Stand (H-7″, D-7″). Circular, concave body. Grey-red pottery. For nos. 162 and 163, see Pl. XII, Fig. 2.

164. Jar with three short legs (H-1′ 8″). Red pottery. Pl. XII, Fig. 4.

165. Jar with three short legs (H-1′, Legs-2½″). Red pottery. Pl. XII, Fig. 3.

166. Jar with three legs (H-1′ 3½″, Legs-5½″). Red pottery coated with lime. Pl. XII, Fig. 5.

167. Jar with three legs (H-1′ 9″, Legs-4″). Similar to no. 166.

LARGE EARTHENWARE SARCOPHAGI.

These are placed in the north-east corner of the gallery. They are generally oblong cists of thick coarse red pottery, rounded at each end and on the cross section of the bottom, and supported by two or three rows of short roughly shaped cylindrical legs. These legs are hollow and sometimes have a hole perforated in the inner side for drainage of moisture.

No cists of this type were found at Tinnevelly, but both these and the pyriform urns occur at Perumbāir. Sometimes they are simply filled with earth and nothing else, others again may have a few bones and pottery, or articles of the latter alone. They have all at one time been covered by an elongated dome-shaped lid, but only two fairly complete examples occur on nos. 171 and 172. The position of the cists was generally marked by stone circles of rough boulders on the surface of the ground, and a low mound which may at one time have been higher than at present.

168. Oval. (L-1′ 9″, B-11½″, H-6″). No legs. Contained nothing but earth.

169. Ovoid. (L-2′ 5″, B-1′ 6½″ at top, and L-3′, B-2′ 2″ at lower part of body, H-2′ 3″, H-of leg-7″). A central longitudinal row of four legs and two side rows of three legs each. It was filled with stiff hard earth. In the upper part were fragments of thick pottery with short cylindrical legs; one of these adhered by clay to the inner side of the cist and has been left in that position. There were also several fragments of human bones including a jaw, which are evidently not the original deposits put into the cist, but belong to a smaller one which had been placed over it and fallen inside. On the bottom of the cist are the bones of a skeleton, with the skull lying at one end. Its position at the opposite end from that in which the jaw-bone lay, is noteworthy and would show that the bones did not belong to one person The skeleton would seem to be nearly complete, but some of the bones are broken, and their appearance indicates that they were so when placed inside. The skull and other bones have been left untouched and lie with the remaining earth in the cist in their original position. The jaw-bone and fragments of bones found in the upper earth have been placed at one end of the cist. The two pottery vessels nos. 20 and 21 were found lying outside one end of this cist. Their position is illustrated in fig. 6, text illustration on page 96 of D.G.'s Annual for 1908-09. Pl. XIII, Figs. 5 and 6.

170. Oblong, rounded at each end. (L-3′, B-1′ 3″, H-1′ 7″, H. of legs-8″). Two rows of four legs each. Roughly moulded rim around the top. Contained nothing but earth. Some pottery, iron implements and bones have been arranged inside, to indicate the way in which such objects were found in the sarcophagi.

171. Oblong, rounded at each end. (L-4′, B-1′6″, H-2′, H-of legs-11″). Two rows of four legs each. Roughly moulded rim with notched ornament around the top. Retains part of the original cover which, though cracked and in pieces, corresponds in length and breadth to the outline of the cist. In cross section the cover is dome-shaped, and round holes about an inch in diameter, are pierced through it at irregular intervals. In order to retain and show the form of the lid the cist has been left unopened.

172. Oblong, rounded at each end. (L-2′ 6″, B-1′ 4″, H-1′ 6″, H-of leg-9″). Two rows of three legs each. Is a smaller form of no. 171. In this case also the cist has been left unopened, so as not to disturb or break the lid.

173. The rounded end part of a broken cist (L-1′ 2″, B-1′2″, H-1′ 1″). Four of the legs remain. On the outside of the rounded end are two raised nearly vertical strips, with crude indented ornament. The cist is filled with a heaped up collection of pottery, comprising pots, stands, lids, etc. These have been left stuck together with hard earth, in the exact position in which they were found.

174. The lower part of a cist, with the sides detached. (L-3′ 4″, B-1′ 7,″ H-9″). Three rows of four legs each. The bones of a skeleton lie in their original position among some adhering earth. At the centre of one end of a broken-off side is a rough ornament representing a turned-up hook, with tassel hanging from it. This fragment is numbered 174 A, and is placed alongside. Pl. XIII, Figs. 2 and 3.

175. Oblong, rounded at each end. (L-6′, B-1′ 10½″, H-1′ 6″, and H-of leg 9″). Two rows of six legs each. Roughly moulded rim with notched ornament around the top. The earth in the . interior was removed and examined, but except a globular vessel with cylindrical neck, which has been left lying in position, nothing else was found. As the cist is fractured in several places, it had to be fixed with wire at the cracks, and the earth filling replaced. Some fragment· ary pieces of a lid were attached to the top of the cist. Pl XIII, Fig. 4.

PLATE I.

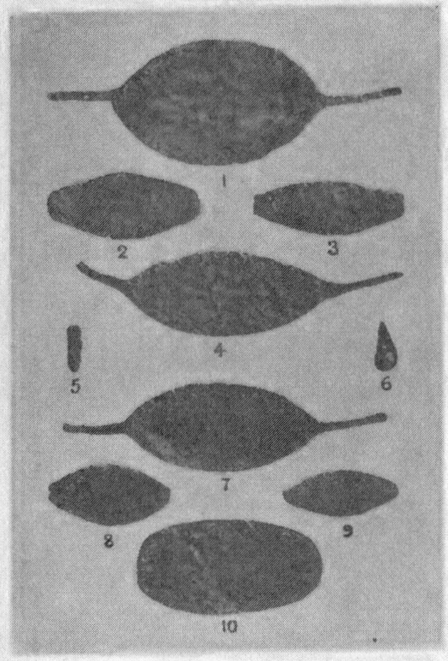

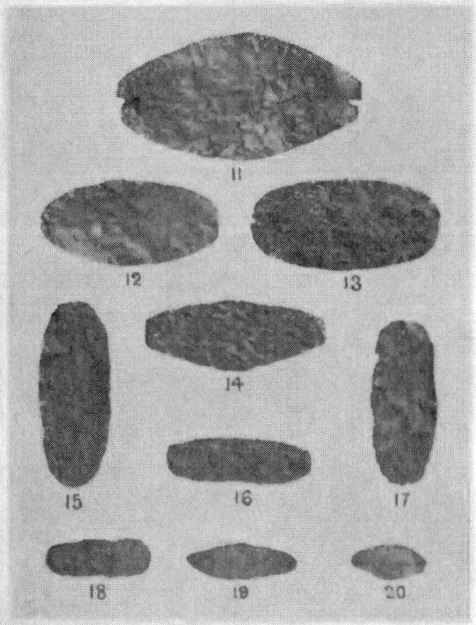

PLATE II.

1
2
3
4
5
6
7
8
9
10
11
12
13
14
15
16
17
18
19
20
21
22
23
24
25
26
27
28
29
30
31
32
33

PLATE III.

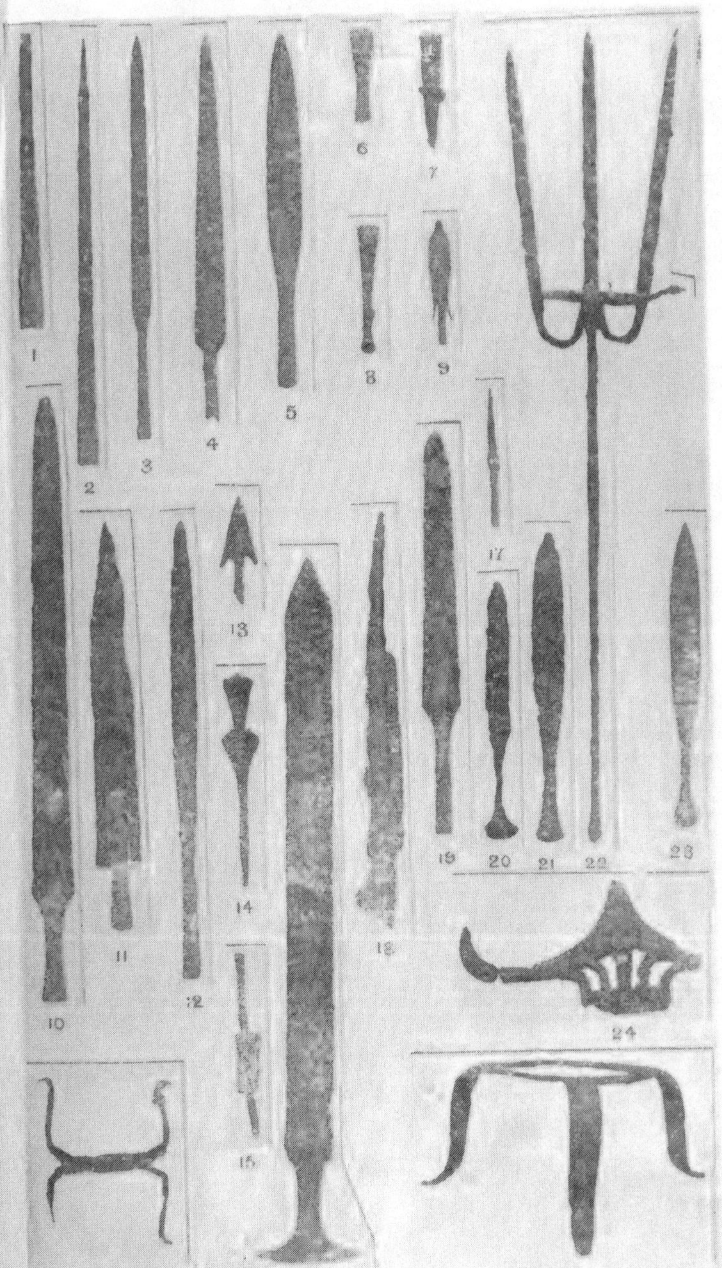

PLATE IV.

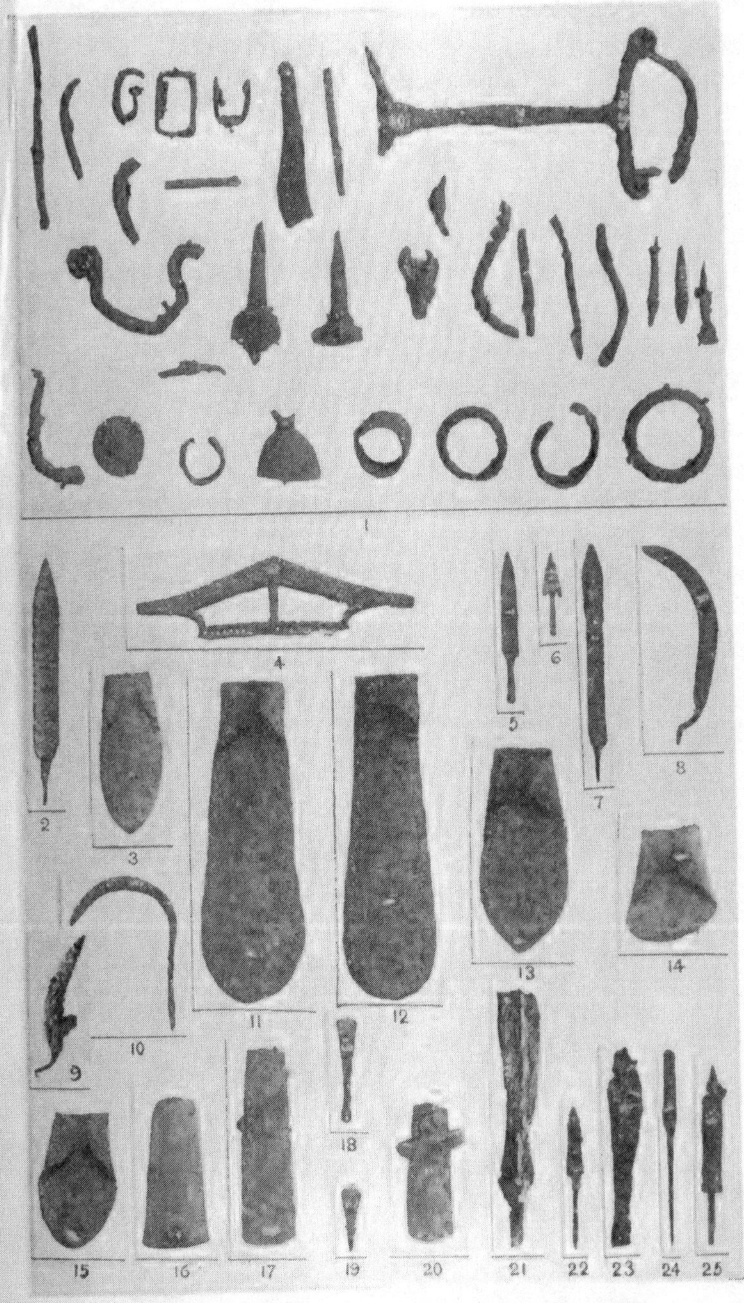

PLATE V.

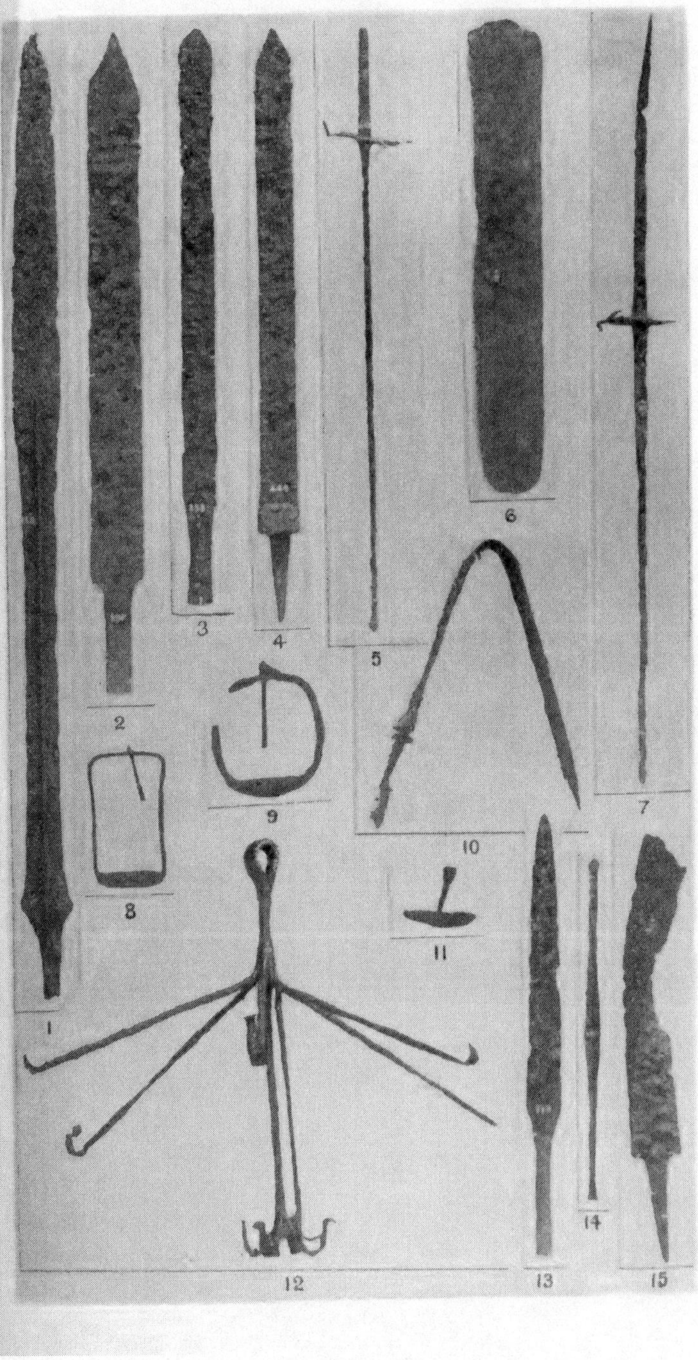

PLATE VI.

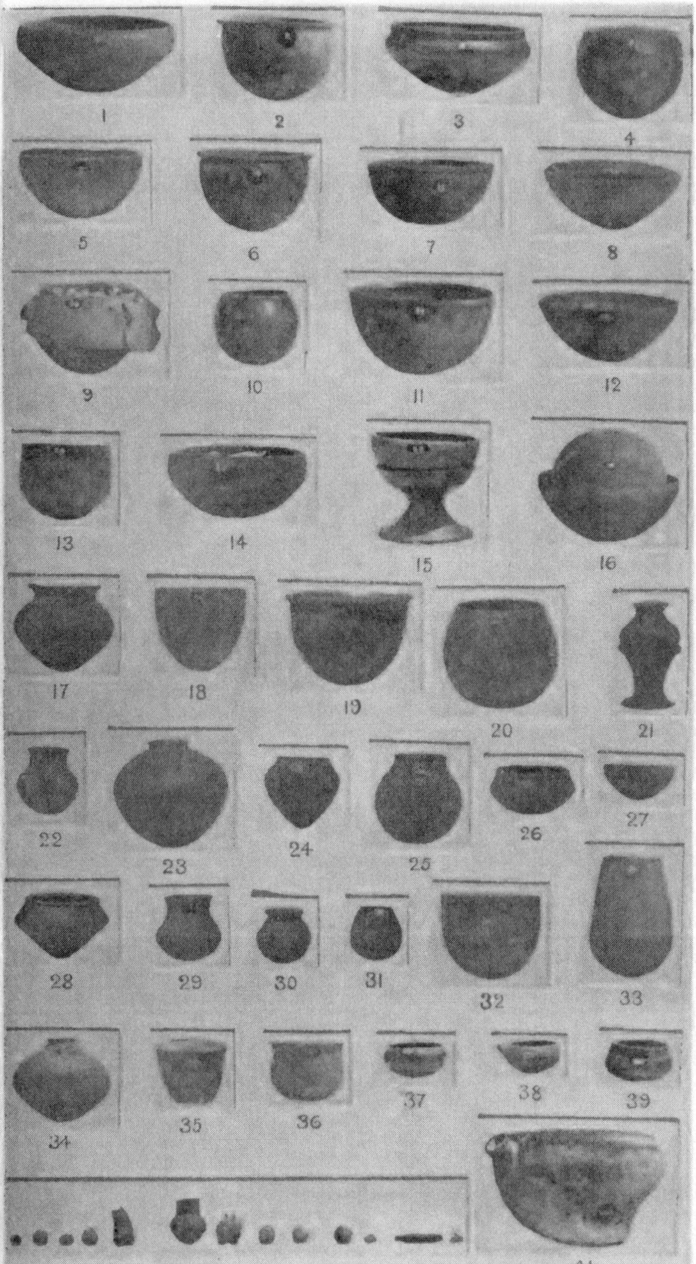

1
2
3
4
5
6
7
8
9
10
11
12
13
14
15
16
17
18
19
20
21
22
23
24
25
26
27
28
29
30
31
32
33
34
35
36
37
38
39
40
41

PLATE VII.

1
2
3
4
5
6
7
8
9
10
11
12
13
14
15
16
17
18
19
20
21
22
23
24
25
26
27
28
29
30
31
32
33
34
35
36
37
38
39

PLATE VIII.

1
2
3
4
5
6
7
8
9
10
11
12
13
14
15
16
17
18
19
20
21
22
23
24
25
26
27
28
29
30

PLATE IX.

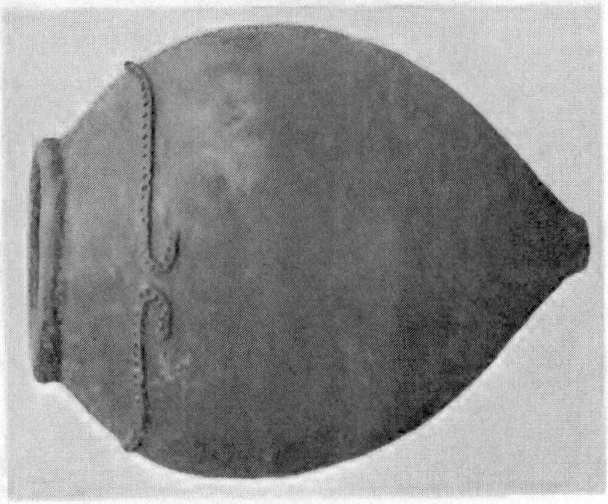

2

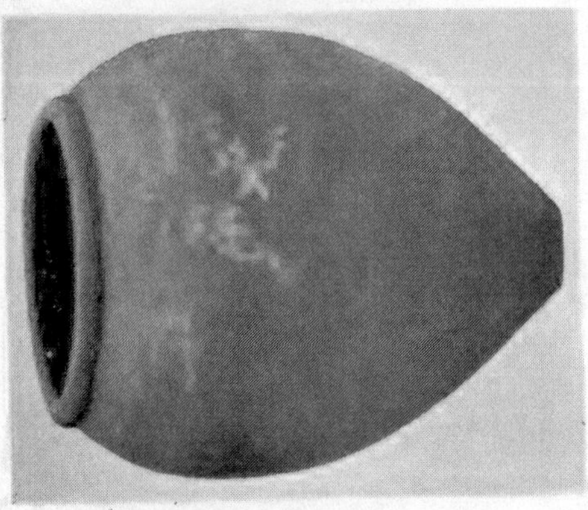

1

PLATE X.

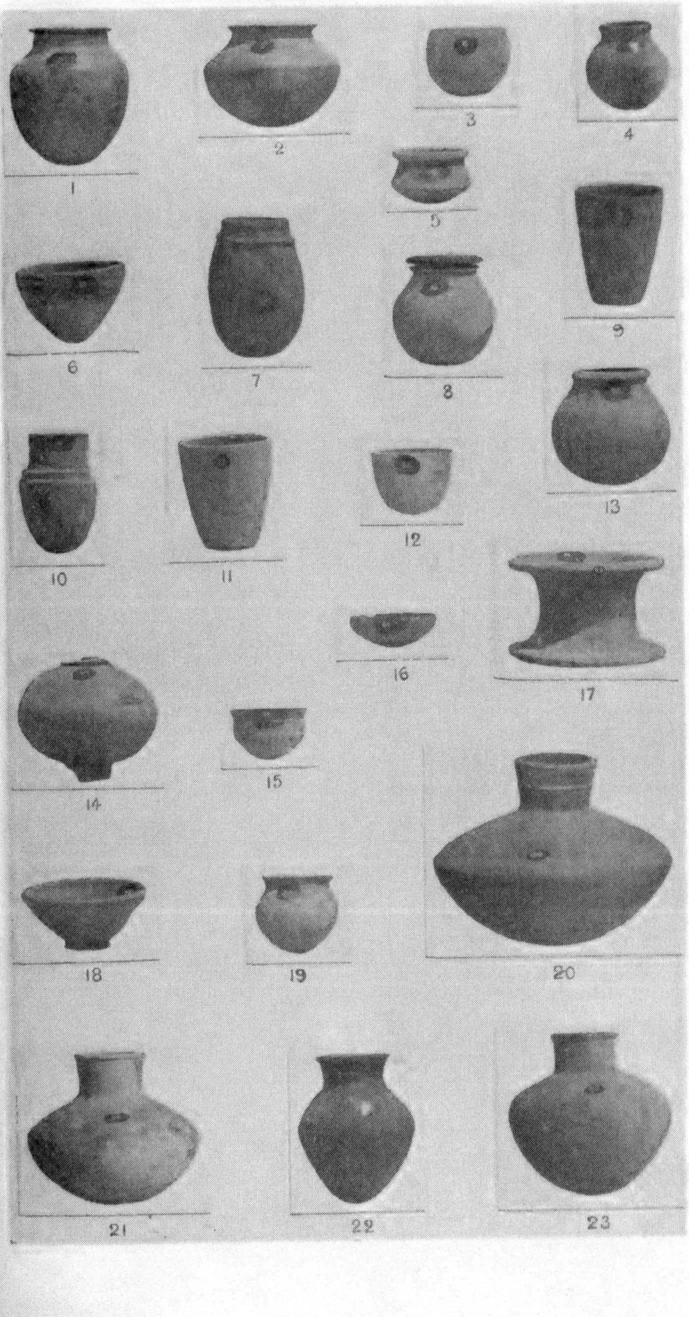

PLATE XI.

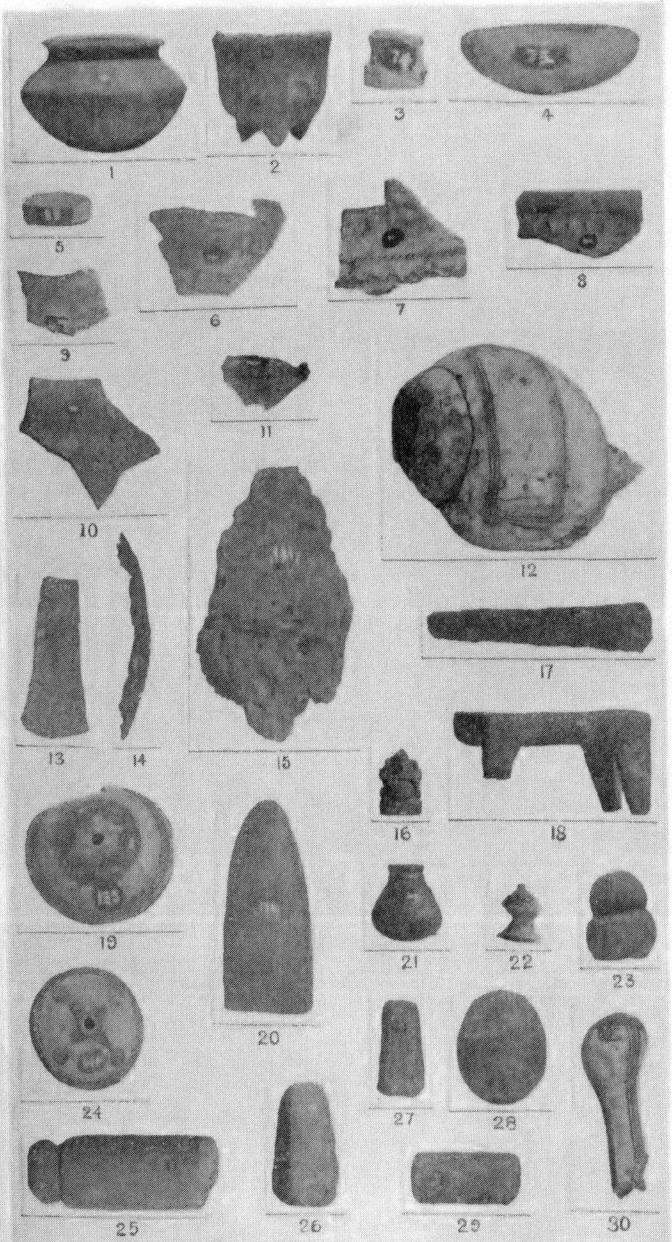

PLATE XII.

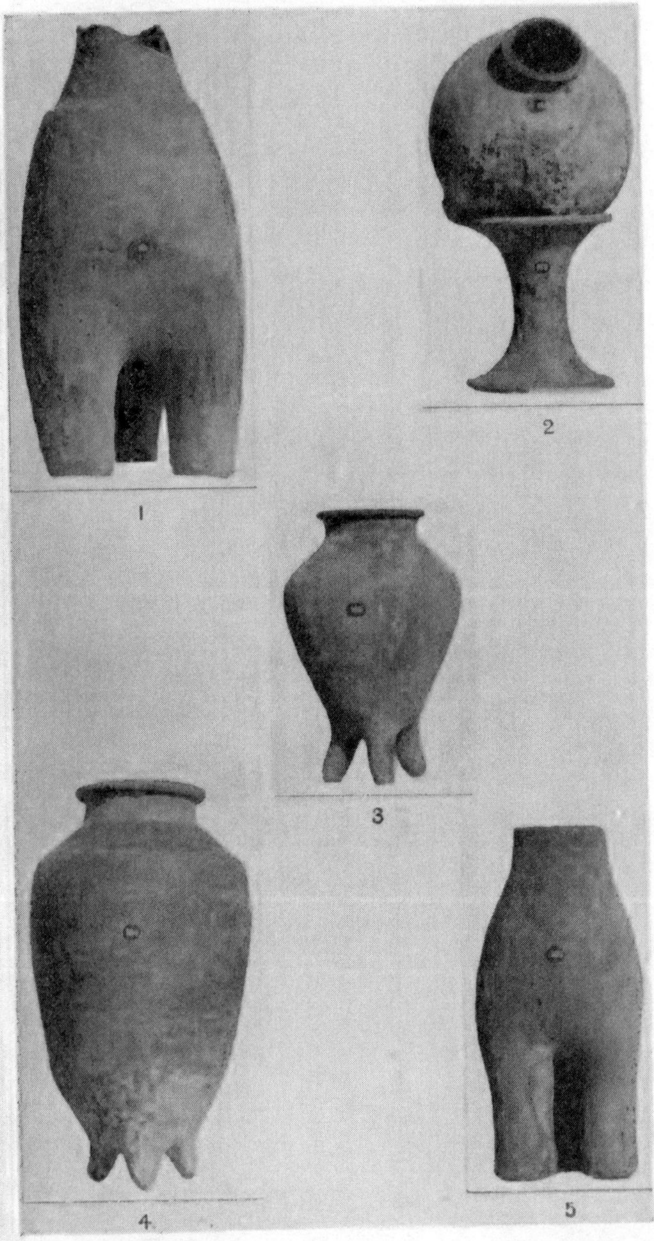

PLATE XIII.

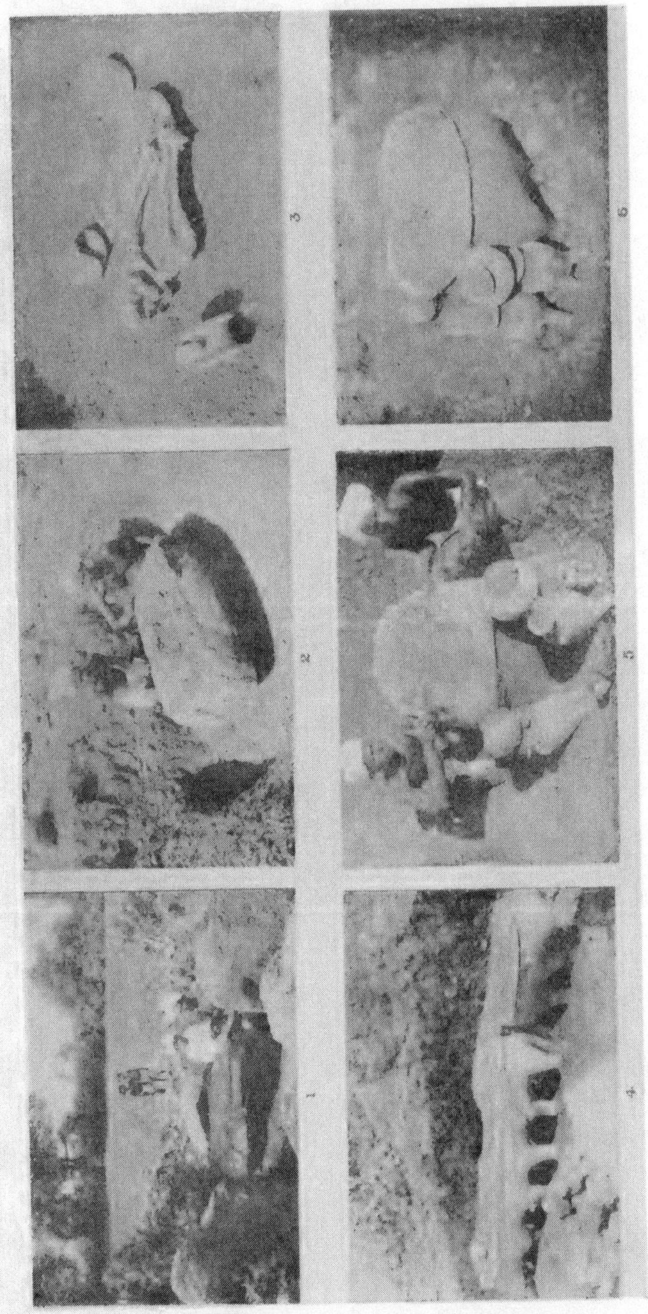